The Word IS The Word DOES

Evelyn Cross and Lynn Harrington

Written Words Publishing LLC
14189 E Dickinson Drive, Unit F
Aurora, CO 80014
www.writtenwordspublishing.com

The Word IS The Word DOES © 2018 by Evelyn Cross and Lynn Harrington.

All rights reserved. No part of this publication may be reproduced, stored in a retrieval system, or transmitted in any form by any means, electronic, mechanical, photocopying, recording, or otherwise, without the prior permission of the author.

Published by Written Words Publishing LLC 9/24/2018

ISBN: 978-0-692-19264-1 (paperback)
ISBN: 979-8-9873088-7-5 (eBook)

Library of Congress Control Number: 2018958162

Cover designed by Tracy L. Bell

Manufactured and printed in the United States of America

"*The Word IS The Word DOES* is a beautifully written tool to help the Body of Christ flourish!"

Written by Reverend Jennifer Kostyal
Founder, Transformed By the Word Ministries
Wilmington, NC

TABLE OF CONTENTS

A Spotlight for Attention to the Word of God vi

Use This Book viii

The Format ix

Receive Jesus as Your Savior ix

Biblical Translations Used xi

Synonyms for the Word of God xiv

The Word IS 1

The Word DOES 62

Index 95

A Spotlight for Attention to the Word of God

"My son, attend to my words; consent and submit to my sayings. Let them not depart from your sight; keep them in the center of your heart. For they are life to those who find them, healing and health to all their flesh" (Proverbs 4:20-22 Amp).

The Word of God is tangible—it IS something and it DOES something. The Word is a person, Jesus Christ, who is at work performing the Will of God, the Father. Whatever the need, the answer is in the Word of God. The Word is the answer and the Word does the answer.

During a time in Evelyn's life of great trial (rejection, hurt, disregard, discard, lack, depression, displacement), she went to the Word of God for relief. As she was studying Psalm 119, God gave her a deep revelation about the Word. His revelations were so profound; she began to write and categorize them.

The purpose for writing this book is to share what God exposed, and continues to reveal, by listing what the WORD IS and what the WORD DOES. When we know the significance of the Word of God (what it IS and what it DOES), we can focus our attention on it and use it effectively.

Are you using the Word or just reading it? Do you need a guide to live by? The intention of this book is to present the active workings of the Word so that we may live by the material, although unseen, Word of God. It is a tool and a reference for life application.

A description of the tangibility of the Word of God is in Rick Warren's popular book, *The Purpose Driven Life*:[1]

"The Spirit of God uses the Word of God to make us like the Son of God. To become like Jesus, we must fill our lives with his Word. The Bible says, '*Through the Word we are put together and shaped up for the tasks God has for us.*' God's Word is unlike any other word. It is alive. When God speaks, things change. Everything around you—all of creation—exists because 'God said it.' He spoke it all into existence. Without God's Word you would not even be alive. James points out, '*God decided to give us life through the Word of truth so we*

---

[1] *Warren, R. (2002). The Purpose Driven Life. Michigan: Zondervan.*

might be the most important of all the things He made.' The Bible is far more than a doctrinal guidebook. God's Word generates life, creates faith, produces change, frightens the devil, causes miracles, heals hurts, builds character, transforms circumstances, imparts joy, overcomes adversity, defeats temptation, infuses hope, releases power, cleanses our minds, brings things into being, and guarantees our future forever! We cannot live without the Word of God! Never take it for granted. You should consider it as essential to your life as food. Job said, *'I have treasured the Words of His mouth more than my daily bread.'* God's Word is the spiritual nourishment you must have to fulfill your purpose. The Bible is called our milk, bread, solid food, and sweet dessert. This four-course meal is the Spirit's menu for spiritual strength and growth. Peter advises us, *'Crave pure spiritual milk, so that by it you may grow up in your salvation.'* God's Word exposes our motives, points out our faults, rebukes our sin, and expects us to change."

The Word of God is tangible; it "IS" and it "DOES." The Word of God is active, alive, accomplishing all God intends, but it will not work for us until we know and use it. This book is for believers (those who have believed and confessed Jesus Christ as Lord) and seekers (those wondering about Jesus and the purpose and value of the Bible). If you are the latter, you need Jesus to receive and understand what the Word IS and what the Word DOES. To receive Him, turn to page ix, **Receive Jesus as Your Savior**.

Reasons to know what the Word IS and what it DOES:
- To know Jesus Christ who is the Word. The Word is the testimony of Jesus Christ (read John 5:39). We know Jesus by knowing the Word.
- To fulfill it, to do it, to obey it.
- To recognize the provision, power, promise, and performance of the Word.
- To honor God's Word as He does. *"I will worship toward Your holy temple and praise Your name for Your loving-kindness and for Your truth and faithfulness; for You have exalted above all else Your name and Your word and You have magnified Your word above all Your name!"* (Psalm 138:2 Amp). The

Jerusalem Bible says, "...your promise is even greater than your fame" and the Living Bible says, "...for your promises are backed by all the honor of your name."

- To know what is ours in Christ; the terms of the agreement He has purchased for us.
- To use its power. God put His power in words, the Bible, and gave it to mankind. *"Who being the brightness of his glory, and the express image of his person, and upholding all things by the word of his power, when he had by himself purged our sins, sat down on the right hand of the Majesty on high:"* (Hebrews 1:3 KJV).
- To correctly speak the Word.
- To get wisdom, knowledge and understanding.

The Word IS everything we need! The Word DOES everything we need! (Read 2 Peter 1:3)

May the Word of the Lord have free course (run, hold its onward course, spread rapidly, speed on, go forward unhindered) and be glorified (honored, extolled, prove its glorious power, triumph) in and through you. As you read the Bible and this book, may the Lord open your eyes to see wonderful truths from His Word.

Use This Book

- As a reference guide for the practical application of God's Word to daily living. When you have a need, find the topic of your need in this book (the index may help), read the scriptures, meditate on the scriptures, believe it, and confess it.
- As a guide for praying the Word for ourselves and others.
- As a daily devotional. Read it for knowledge of what the Word IS and what the Word DOES.
- As a tool for scripture memorization and meditation.
- As a training tool for ministers and leaders.
- As an instructional tool when teaching students how to use and the meaning of the Bible. It is useable in Bible study, Bible classes, Christian schools and home schooling.
- For reference when questioned about the Bible.

The Format

Sections of this book state what the Word IS and what the Word DOES in alphabetical order for ease of use and reference. They list and describe:
1. <u>The Word IS and The Word DOES</u>: Lists various topics that are identified in God's Word.
2. <u>Scripture</u>: Biblical reference for what the Word IS and what the Word DOES quoted from several biblical translations. Some scriptures are written in part to state the text that directly supports what God's Word IS or God's Word DOES. In these instances, the KJV is written in full for understanding the translation written in part, although the KJV may not directly state what the Word IS or what the Word DOES. Feel free to refer to your favorite Bible version.
3. <u>Revelation, Meaning, Comments, Examples, Supporting Scriptures</u>: Used to add further knowledge and understanding for some topics, as revealed to the authors. Record your own revelation and comments in the margins.

Receive Jesus as Your Savior
(Taken from the book *Spirit, Soul & Body* by Andrew Wommack).[2]

Choosing to receive Jesus Christ as your Lord and Savior is the most important decision you'll ever make! God's Word promises, "That if thou shalt confess with thy mouth the Lord Jesus, and shalt believe in thine heart that God hath raised him from the dead, thou shalt be saved. For with the heart man believeth unto righteousness; and with the mouth confession is made unto salvation…For whosoever shall call upon the name of the Lord shall be saved" (Romans 10:9-10,13 KJV).

By His grace, God has already done everything to provide salvation. Your part is simply to believe and receive.

Pray out loud, "Jesus, I confess that You are my Lord and Savior. I believe in my heart that God raised You from the

---

[2] *Wommack, A. (2010). Spirit, Soul & Body. Oklahoma: Harrison House Publishers.*

dead. By faith in Your Word, I receive salvation now. Thank You for saving me!"

    The very moment you commit your life to Jesus Christ the truth of His Word instantly comes to pass in your spirit. Now that you're born again, there's a brand new you!

Biblical Translations Used

Several versions (translations) of the Bible are used in this book. Most of the translations are taken from *The WORD, The Bible From 26 Translations,* Curtis Vaughn, Th.D. General Editor, 1988 Mathis Publishers, Inc. The translation is abbreviated at the end of the scripture. The translations used are identified by the following abbreviations. If there are two translations with the same abbreviation but with different titles, NT denotes the version used for New Testament scriptures.

AAT	The Bible: An American Translation (J.M. Powis Smith and Edgar J. Goodspeed)
ABPS	The Holy Bible Containing the Old and New Testaments: An Improved Edition (American Baptist Publication Society)
ABUV	The New Testament of Our Lord and Savior Jesus Christ, American Bible Union Version (John A. Broadus et al)
Alf	The New Testament (Henry Alford)
Amp	The Amplified Bible
AmpNT	The Amplified New Testament
ASV	The American Standard Version
Bas	The Bible in Basic English
BasNT	The New Testament in Basic English
Beck	The New Testament in the Language of Today (William F. Beck)
Ber	The Modern Language Bible: The New Berkeley Version in Modern English
BerNT	The Berkeley Version of the New Testament (Gerrit Verkuyl)
Con	The Epistles of Paul (W.J. Conybeare)
DeW	Praise-Songs of Israel: A Rendering of the Book of Psalms (John DeWitt)
Gspd	The New Testament: An American Translation (Edgar J. Goodspeed)
Har	The Psalms for Today: A New Translation from the Hebrew into Current English (R.K. Harrison)
Jerus	The Jerusalem Bible
JPS	The Holy Scriptures According to the Masoretic Text: A New Translation (The Jewish Publication Society)

The Word IS The Word DOES

KJV	King James Version
Knox	The Holy Bible: A Translation from the Latin Vulgate in the Light of the Hebrew and Greek Originals (Monsignor Ronald Knox)
KnoxNT	The New Testament in the Translation of Monsignor Ronald Knox
Lam	The Holy Bible from Ancient Eastern Manuscripts (George M. Lamsa)
LamNT	The New Testament According to the Eastern Texts (George M. Lamsa)
Mof	A New Translation of the Bible (James Moffatt)
MofNT	The New Testament: A New Translation (James Moffatt)
Mon	The Centenary Translation: The New Testament in Modern English (Helen Barrett Montgomery)
NAB	The New American Bible
NASB	The New American Standard Bible
NEB	The New English Bible
NEBNT	The New English Bible: New Testament
NIV	New International Version
NKJV	New King James Version
Nor	The New Testament: A New Translation (Olaf M. Norlie)
PBV	The Psalms in the Book of Common Prayer of the Anglican Church
Phi	Four Prophets: Amos, Hosea, First Isaiah, Micah (J.B. Phillips)
PhiNT	The New Testament in Modern English (J.B. Phillips)
Rieu	The Four Gospels (E.V. Rieu) The Book of the Acts (C.H. Rieu)
Rhm	The Emphasized Bible: A New Translation (J.B. Rotherham)
RhmNT	The Emphasized New Testament: A New Translation (J.B. Rotherham)
RSV	The Revised Standard Version
RV	The Holy Bible: Revised Version
Sept	The Septuagint (Charles Thomson)
Sprl	A Translation of the Old Testament Scriptures from the Original Hebrew (Helen Spurrell)
Tay	The Living Bible: Paraphrased (Kenneth Taylor)

TayNT	Living Letter: The Paraphrased Epistles (Kenneth Taylor)
	Living Gospels: The Paraphrased Gospels (Kenneth Taylor)
	Living Prophecies: The Minor Prophets Paraphrased (Kenneth Taylor)
	Daniel and the Revelation (Kenneth N. Taylor)
TCNT	The Twentieth Century New Testament
Tor	The Torah: The Five Books of Moses
Wey	The New Testament in Modern Speech (Richard Francis Weymouth)
Wms	The New Testament: A Translation in the Language of the People (Charles B. Williams)
YLT	Young's Literal Translation of the Holy Bible (Robert Young)

Synonyms for the Word of God

Code (Deuteronomy 17:18, 27:26, 31:11)
- A set of rules about how something should be done or how people should behave

Commandment (Psalm 19:6; 1 John 2:7-8)
- Eternal's command, order, Divine orders
- NT - That which is imposed by decree or law; injunction, charge, precept, a commission, a proclamation

Judgments (Deuteronomy 11:32)
- God's judicial decisions, ordinances, Eternal's rulings
- NT - A separating decision, a decision passed on the faults of others, an ordinance, a sentence, condemnation

Law (Psalm 19:1)
- Torah, direction, instruction, teaching

Oracles (Romans 3:2; 1 Peter 4:11)
- A message believed to come from God
- A wise or prophetic statement

Ordinances (Psalm 119:43)
- NT - Decree, disposition, creation/creature, tradition

Precepts (Psalm 19:4)
- A commandment

Scriptures (Romans 1:2; 2 Timothy 3:15; 1 Corinthians 15:3; Luke 4:21, 24:27,45)
- A passage from the Bible
- The sacred writings of the Bible

Statutes (Psalm 19:5; Deuteronomy 11:32)
- OT - Prescription, rule, law, regulation (derived from the verb haqaq: to cut in, determine, decree), portion (something due as an allowance or payment)

Testimony (Psalm 19:2)
- NT - Witness, a bearing witness, a declaration of facts

The Word IS The Word DOES

- OT - Refers to the Ten Commandments as a solemn divine charge or duty; "tables of testimony", "ark of the testimony", "tabernacle (housing for the ark) of testimony"; the entire law of God

The Word IS

Abiding

"….the living and abiding word of God" (1 Peter 1:23 RSV).

"I have written unto you, fathers, because ye have known him that is from the beginning. I have written unto you, young men, because ye are strong, and the word of God abideth in you, and ye have overcome the wicked one" (1 John 2:14 KJV).

Advisor

"my advisers are thine own injunctions—I delight in them" (Psalm 119:24 Mof).

Agreement

"He has kept his agreement in mind for ever, the word which he gave for a thousand generations;" (1 Chronicles 16:15 Bas).

Beautiful

"All who were present spoke well of him and were astonished at the beautiful words that fell from his lips" (Luke 4:22 TCNT).

"and learnt to appreciate the beauty of the Divine Message…" (Hebrews 6:5 TCNT).

Blessing to Those Who Keep It

"Blessed are they that keep His testimonies, and that seek Him with the whole heart" (Psalm 119:2 KJV).

"But he said, Yea rather, blessed are they that hear the word of God, and keep it" (Luke 11:28 KJV).

"But whoso looketh into the perfect law of liberty, and continueth therein, he being not a forgetful hearer, but a doer of the work, this man shall be blessed in his deed" (James 1:25 KJV).

The Word IS The Word DOES

The Word IS

"...keeps on looking..." (Wms).

"Blessed is he that readeth, and they that hear the words of this prophecy, and keep those things which are written therein: for the time is at hand" (Revelation 1:3 KJV).

<u>Revelation, Meaning, Comments, Examples, Supporting Scriptures</u>:

Keeping the Word means we do the Word, we live in obedience to the Word, we apply it to our lives, we make it the standard we live by. *"But be ye doers of the word, and not hearers only, deceiving your own selves. For if any be a hearer of the word, and not a doer, he is like unto a man beholding his natural face in a glass: For he beholdeth himself, and goeth his way, and straightway forgetteth what manner of man he was"* (James 1:22-24 KJV).

Blessing to Those Who Read and Hear It

"Blessed is he that readeth, and they that hear the words of this prophecy..." (Revelation 1:3 KJV).

Blessing to Those Who Seek Him with the Whole Heart

"Blessed are they that keep His testimonies, and that seek Him with the whole heart" (Psalm 119:2 KJV).

<u>Revelation, Meaning, Comments, Examples, Supporting Scriptures</u>:

A whole heart is an undivided heart, all your heart. *"Happy are they who follow his injunctions, giving him undivided hearts"* (Psalm 119:2 Mof).

The blessing is God Himself. *"And you will be searching for me and I will be there, when you have gone after me with all your heart"* (Jeremiah 29:13 Bas).

The Word IS

Blessing to Those Who Walk in It

"Blessed are the undefiled in the way, who walk in the law of the Lord" (Psalm 119:1 KJV).

> *"Blessed (happy, fortunate, to be envied) are the undefiled (the upright, truly sincere, and blameless) in the way [of the revealed will of God], who walk (order their conduct and conversation) in the law of the Lord (the whole of God's revealed will)"* (Amp).

Revelation, Meaning, Comments, Examples, Supporting Scriptures:

"Blessed (happy, blithesome, joyous, spiritually prosperous—with life-joy and satisfaction in God's favor and salvation, regardless of their outward conditions)..." (Matthew 5:5 AmpNT).

The blessing of this scripture is conditional upon obedience; living in Christ.

Book of the Law, Book of the Lord, Book of Prophecy

"And he read therein before the street that was before the water gate from the morning until midday, before the men and the women, and those that could understand; and the ears of all the people were attentive unto the book of the law" (Nehemiah 8:3 KJV).

"Seek ye out of the book of the Lord, and read: no one of these shall fail, none shall want her mate: for my mouth it hath commanded, and his spirit it hath gathered them" (Isaiah 34:16 KJV).

> *"Turn back, when the time comes, to this record of divine prophecy, and read it afresh: you shall learn, then, that none of these signs are lacking, none waited for the coming of the next..."* (Knox).

"For as many as are of the works of the law are under the curse: for it is written, Cursed is every one that continueth not

The Word IS

in all things which are written in the book of the law to do them" (Galatians 3:10 KJV).

"And if any man shall take away from the words of the book of this prophecy, God shall take away his part out of the book of life, and out of the holy city, and from the things which are written in this book" (Revelation 22:19 KJV).

Revelation, Meaning, Comments, Examples, Supporting Scriptures:

The entire Word of God prophesies to us, tells of the life of Christ and is life to us. Are we attentive to hearing the Word?

The Book of the Law refers to the Word of God. The law of the Lord is the whole of God's revealed will. We do not currently live under the law, but under grace. Christ Himself said He did not come to do away with the law, but to fulfill it. Therefore, all the scripture applies to our lives.

Broad

"I have seen that everything [human] has its limits and end [no matter how extensive, noble, and excellent]; but Your commandment is exceedingly broad and extends without limits [into eternity]" (Psalm 119:96 Amp).

Revelation, Meaning, Comments, Examples, Supporting Scriptures:

God's Word is limitless, boundless (like Him). It is exceedingly broad.

Cause for Praise, Songs, Rejoicing

"I will praise thee with uprightness of heart, when I shall have learned thy righteous judgments" (Psalm 119:7 KJV).

The Word IS

"My hands also will I lift up unto thy commandments, which I have loved; and I will meditate in thy statutes" (Psalm 119:48 KJV).

"Thy statutes have been my songs in the house of my pilgrimage" (Psalm 119:54 KJV).

"I rejoice at thy word, as one that findeth great spoil" (Psalm 119:162 KJV).

"Seven times a day do I praise thee because of thy righteous judgments" (Psalm 119:164 KJV).

"My lips shall utter praise, when thou hast taught me thy statutes" (Psalm 119:171 KJV).

"Let my soul live, and it shall praise thee; and let thy judgments help me" (Psalm 119:175 KJV).
   "May I live to praise You…" (Har).

Revelation, Meaning, Comments, Examples, Supporting Scriptures:

Hearing His Word reveals who He is which causes me to praise. God's Word is my praise. The Word is a treasure I have found which causes me to praise. We live to praise Him.

Clear

"…the Eternal's command is clear, a light to the mind" (Psalm 19:8 Mof).
   "…The commandment of the Lord shines clear and gives light to the eyes" (NEB).

Revelation, Meaning, Comments, Examples, Supporting Scriptures:

His Word is uncontaminated.

The Word IS

Code

"...he must write for himself in a book a copy of this code as approved by the Levitical priests" (Deuteronomy 17:18 AAT).
"...he must have a copy of this code written for himself, taken from the copy in charge of the priestly Levites" (Mof).

"...who does not give effect to the provisions of this code by observing them..." (Deuteronomy 27:26 AAT).

"...you must read this code aloud in the hearing of all Israel" (Deuteronomy 31:11 Mof).

<u>Revelation, Meaning, Comments, Examples, Supporting Scriptures</u>:

Thank God for Jesus Christ who kept the law and became a curse for us because we could not.

Comfort

"This is my comfort and consolation in my affliction; That Your word has revived me and given me life" (Psalm 119:50 Amp).

"I remembered thy judgments of old, O Lord; and have comforted myself" (Psalm 119:52 KJV).

"Let, I pray thee, thy merciful kindness be for my comfort, according to thy word unto thy servant" (Psalm 119:76 KJV).

"Unless thy law had been my comfort, I would have died in my misery" (Psalm 119:92 Mof).

<u>Revelation, Meaning, Comments, Examples, Supporting Scriptures</u>:

The Word is strength, refreshing, reviving in all troubles. It gives life. We would perish without the Word of God. Everything would fail without the Word.

The Word IS

Comforting

"And the Lord answered the angel that talked with me with good words and comfortable words" (Zechariah 1:13 KJV).

"And the Lord answered gracious and comforting words to the angel who talked with me" (RSV).

"...with favourable words and with comfortable words" (Sprl).

"And with that, the Lord answered him; gracious his words were, gracious and full of comfort" (Knox).

Commandment

"And the Lord said unto Moses, Come up to me into the mount, and be there: and I will give thee tables of stone, and a law, and commandments which I have written..." (Exodus 24:12 KJV).

"If any man think himself to be a prophet, or spiritual, let him acknowledge that the things that I write unto you are the commandments of the Lord" (1 Corinthians 14:37 KJV).

"Brethren, I write no new commandment unto you, but an old commandment which ye had from the beginning. The old commandment is the word which ye have heard from the beginning" (1 John 2:7 KJV).

Compact

"Then he took the scroll of the compact..." (Exodus 24:7 Mof).

"Never forget his compact, the pledge he gave for a thousand generations" (1 Chronicles 16:15 Mof).

Complete

"The law of Yahweh is complete..." (Psalm 19:7 Rhm).

The Word IS

Consoling

"And Yahweh answered the messenger who was speaking to me in words that were pleasant, words that were consoling" (Zechariah 1:13 Rhm).

Content of My Heart

"Thy word have I hid in mine heart, that I might not sin against thee" (Psalm 119:11 KJV).
> "Thy word have I laid up in my heart, That I might not sin against thee" (ASV).

Revelation, Meaning, Comments, Examples, Supporting Scriptures:

The Word is what I own, my property, something that has been given to me.

Counsellors

"Thy testimonies also are my delight and my counsellors" (Psalm 119:24 KJV).

Course, Way, Pattern for Living

"I will run the way of thy commandments, when thou shalt enlarge my heart" (Psalm 119:32 KJV).
> "I will follow Your pattern for living, for You give me increasing discernment" (Har).
> "I will run the course set out in thy commandments, for they gladden my heart" (NEB).

Covenant

"And...the book he had written—the Book of the Covenant—containing God's directions and laws..." (Exodus 24:7 Tay).

The Word IS

"Be ye mindful always of his covenant; the word which he commanded to a thousand generations;" (1 Chronicles 16:15 KJV).

"As for me, this is my covenant with them, saith the Lord; My spirit that is upon thee, and my words which I have put in thy mouth, shall not depart out of thy mouth, nor out of the mouth of thy seed, nor out of the mouth of thy seed's seed, saith the Lord, from henceforth and for ever" (Isaiah 59:21 KJV).

Delight

"I will delight myself in thy statutes: I will not forget thy word" (Psalm 119:16 KJV).
　　"In thy statutes I find continual delight" (NEB).

"Your unchanging word is my delight, and the guide of my footsteps" (Psalm 119:24 Bas).

"Make me to go in the path of thy commandments; for therein do I delight" (Psalm 119:35 KJV).

"And I will delight myself in thy commandments, which I have loved" (Psalm 119:47 KJV).

"Let thy tender mercies come unto me, that I may live: for thy law is my delight" (Psalm 119:77 KJV).

"Unless thy law had been my delights, I should then have perished in mine affliction" (Psalm 119:92 KJV).

"Trouble and anguish have taken hold on me: yet thy commandments are my delights" (Psalm 119:143 KJV).

"I have longed for thy salvation, O Lord; and thy law is my delight" (Psalm 119:174 KJV).

"When Your words came, I devoured them; your word was my delight and the joy of my heart…" (Jeremiah 15:16 Jerus).

The Word IS

"Thy words were found, and I ate them, and thy words became to me a joy and the delight of my heart…" (RSV).
"Your words are what sustained me; they are food to my hungry soul. They bring joy to my sorrowing heart and delight to me…" (Tay).

<u>Revelation, Meaning, Comments, Examples, Supporting Scriptures</u>:

The law is my happiness.

"Show some sympathy towards me, that I may survive, for Your law is my happiness" (Psalm 119:77 Har).

"If Your law had not been my source of happiness, I should long ago have been engulfed by my miseries" (Psalm 119:92 Har).

Deliverance

"Let my supplication come before thee: deliver me according to thy word" (Psalm 119:170 KJV).

Desired More than Gold

"More to be desired are they than gold, yea, than much fine gold: sweeter also than honey and the honeycomb" (Psalm 19:10 KJV).
   "All these are more precious than gold, than a hoard of pure gold…" (Knox).
   "They are more precious than gold, than a heap of purest gold…" (NAB).

<u>Revelation, Meaning, Comments, Examples, Supporting Scriptures</u>:

"I will worship toward Your holy temple and praise Your name for Your loving-kindness and for Your truth and faithfulness; for You have exalted above all else Your name and Your word

The Word IS

and You have magnified Your word above all Your name!" (Psalm 138:2 Amp).

Because the Word of God is magnified above the Name of God, I desire it more than any material thing.

Discerner

"For the word of God is quick, and powerful, and sharper than any twoedged sword, piercing even to the dividing asunder of soul and spirit, and of the joints and marrow, and is a discerner of the thoughts and intents of the heart" (Hebrews 4:12 KJV).

Divine

"The Logos existed in the very beginning, the Logos was with God, the Logos was divine" (John 1:1 MofNT).
   "...the Word was divine" (Gspd).

"and learnt to appreciate the beauty of the Divine Message..." (Hebrews 6:5 TCNT).

<u>Revelation, Meaning, Comments, Examples, Supporting Scriptures</u>:

The Word is divine because the Word is God.

Divinely-inspired

"All Scripture is divinely inspired, and useful..." (2 Timothy 3:16 Gspd).

Effectual

"For the Word of God is living, and effectual..." (Hebrews 4:12 ABUV).

Enduring

"...by God's living and enduring word" (1 Peter 1:23 Wey).

The Word IS

Energetic

"For living is the word of God and energetic…" (Hebrews 4:12 RhmNT).

Engrafted

"Wherefore lay apart all filthiness and superfluity of naughtiness, and receive with meekness the engrafted word, which is able to save your souls" (James 1:21 KJV).
   "…make a soil of humble modesty for the Word which roots itself inwardly" (MofNT).

Revelation, Meaning, Comments, Examples, Supporting Scriptures:

Pride cannot produce soil for the Word.

Ennobling

"have felt the ennobling word of God…" (Hebrews 6:5 BerNT).

Revelation, Meaning, Comments, Examples, Supporting Scriptures:

Ennobling means to make something or someone better or more worthy of admiration.

The Word makes us better. The Word is exalted and elevated above everyone and everything because Jesus is highly exalted.

Established

"Your decrees are firmly established…" (Psalm 93:5 Har).

Eternal (Forever)

"Concerning thy testimonies, I have known of old that thou hast founded them for ever" (Psalm 119:152 KJV).

The Word IS The Word DOES

The Word IS

"Thy word is true from the beginning: and every one of thy righteous judgments endureth for ever" (Psalm 119:160 KJV).
   "…and your upright decision is unchanging for ever" (Bas).

"The grass withereth, the flower fadeth: but the word of our God shall stand for ever" (Isaiah 40:8 KJV).

"Heaven and earth shall pass away: but my words shall not pass away" (Mark 13:31 KJV).

"Heaven and earth shall pass away: but my words shall not pass away" (Luke 21:33 KJV).

"But the word of the Lord endureth forever. And this is the word which by the gospel is preached unto you" (1 Peter 1:25 KJV).
   "But the word of the Lord lives on forever…" (Wms).

Revelation, Meaning, Comments, Examples, Supporting Scriptures:

The Word:
- Is valid for all times. *"…thy decrees are valid for all time"* (Psalm 119:152 Mof).
- Is ordained everlastingly. *"…thou hast ordained them everlastingly"* (Psalm 119:152 Knox).
- *"…cannot be set aside"* (John 10:35 Gspd).
- *"…cannot be annulled"* (John 10:35 Mon).
- *"…cannot be set aside or cancelled or broken or annulled"* (John 10:35 Amp).

Exalted

"…for thou hast exalted above everything thy name and thy word" (Psalm 138:2 RSV).

The Word IS

<u>Revelation, Meaning, Comments, Examples, Supporting Scriptures</u>:

"...for your promises are backed by all the honor of your name" (Psalm 138:2 Tay).

Examples

"Now all these things happened unto them for examples: and they are written for our admonition, upon whom the ends of the world are come" (1 Corinthians 10:11 KJV).
   "Now these things which happened to our ancestors are illustrations of the way in which God works..." (PhiNT).

Faithful

"...The testimony of the Lord is faithful..." (Psalm 19:7 Sept).

"...The decisions of Yahweh are faithful. They are righteous altogether" (Psalm 19:9 Rhm).

"All thy commandments are faithful..." (Psalm 119:86 KJV).
   "Your commandments epitomise faithfulness..." (Jerus).

"Thy testimonies that thou hast commanded are righteous and very faithful" (Psalm 119:138 KJV).
   "Strict justice and utter faithfulness inspire all thy decrees" (Knox).

"Holding fast the faithful word as he hath been taught, that he may be able by sound doctrine both to exhort and to convince the gainsayers" (Titus 1:9 KJV).

<u>Revelation, Meaning, Comments, Examples, Supporting Scriptures</u>:

The Word is sure, steadfast and lasts age after age.

The Word IS

Favourable

"...with favourable words and with comfortable words" (Zechariah 1:13 Sprl).

Fire

"Wherefore thus saith the Lord God of hosts, Because ye speak this word, behold, I will make my words in thy mouth fire, and this people wood, and it shall devour them" (Jeremiah 5:14 KJV).

"Is not My word like fire [that consumes all that cannot endure the test]? says the Lord, and like a hammer that breaks in pieces the rock [of most stubborn resistance]?" (Jeremiah 23:29 Amp).
"Do not my words scorch like fire? says the Lord. Are they not like a hammer that splinters rock?" (NEB).

<u>Revelation, Meaning, Comments, Examples, Supporting Scriptures</u>:

When Jesus explained the scriptures, it was like fire in the hearts of men. "...Did we not feel our hearts on fire..." (Luke 24:32 NEBNT).

Flawless

"As for God, his way is perfect: The Lord's word is flawless; he shields all who take refuge in him" (Psalm 18:30 NIV).

"Every word of God is flawless; he is a shield to those who take refuge in him" (Proverbs 30:5 NIV).

Flesh

"And the Word was made flesh, and dwelt among us, (and we beheld his glory, the glory as of the only begotten of the Father,) full of grace and truth" (John 1:14 KJV).
"...became flesh..." (RhmNT).

The Word IS

"...became a human being..." (PhiNT).

<u>Revelation, Meaning, Comments, Examples, Supporting Scriptures</u>:

Jesus, The Word, was made flesh. *"...and the Word was God"* (John 1:1 KJV).

Food (Bread, Milk, Nourishment)

"Your words are what sustained me; they are food to my hungry soul. They bring joy to my sorrowing heart and delight me. How proud I am to bear Your name, O Lord" (Jeremiah 15:16 Tay).

"But He answered and said, "It is written, 'Man shall not live by bread alone, but by every word that proceeds from the mouth of God'" (Matthew 4:4 NKJV).

"...who have known the wholesome nourishment of the Word of God..." (Hebrews 6:5 PhiNT).

"as newborn babes, desire the pure milk of the word, that you may grow thereby," (1 Peter 2:2 NKJV).

<u>Revelation, Meaning, Comments, Examples, Supporting Scriptures</u>:

It is more needful than food according to Job 23:12 NKJV, "I have treasured the words of His mouth More than my necessary food."

"I gave you milk to drink, not solid food; for you were not yet able to receive it. Indeed, even now you are not yet able," (1 Corinthians 3:2 NASB).

Fulfilled in Jesus Christ

"Think not that I am come to destroy the law, or the prophets: I am not come to destroy, but to fulfil" (Matthew 5:17 KJV).

The Word IS

"...I have not come to annul them, but to give them their completion" (Wey).
"...but to enforce them" (Gspd).
"...but to bring them to perfection" (KnoxNT).

Revelation, Meaning, Comments, Examples, Supporting Scriptures:

Jesus has satisfied, completed, perfected, and enforced every requirement of the law.

Genuine

"...the ordinances of the Lord are genuine and perfectly just" (Psalm 19:9 Har).

God (Logos, Divine, Christ)

"In the beginning [before all time] was the Word (Christ), and the Word was with God, and the Word was God Himself" (John 1:1 AmpNT).
   "In the beginning was the Word, and the Word was with God, and the Word was God" (KJV).
   "...the Logos was with God, the Logos was divine" (MofNT).
   "...was God Himself" (Wms).
   "...what God was, the Word was" (NEBNT).

"And the Word (Christ) became flesh (human, incarnate) and tabernacled (fixed His tent of flesh, lived awhile) among us; and we [actually] saw His glory (His honor, His majesty), such glory as an only begotten son receives from his father, full of grace (favor, loving-kindness) and truth" (John 1:14 AmpNT).

"[We are writing] about the Word of Life [in] Him Who existed from the beginning, Whom we have heard, Whom we have seen with our [own] eyes, Whom we have gazed upon [for ourselves] and have touched with our [own] hands" (1 John 1:1 AmpNT).

The Word IS

"And he was clothed with a vesture dipped in blood: and his name is called The Word of God" (Revelation 19:13 KJV).

Revelation, Meaning, Comments, Examples, Supporting Scriptures:

The Word is one God because the Father, the Word (Jesus Christ) and the Holy Ghost are one. *"For there are three that bear record in heaven, the Father, the Word, and the Holy Ghost: and these three are one"* (1 John 5:7 KJV).

The Word is tangible:
- something that has a physical form (God is a person).
- capable of being understood and evaluated, and therefore regarded as real.

God-breathed

"Every scripture [is] God-breathed, And profitable..." (2 Timothy 3:16 RhmNT).

God-inspired

"Every Scripture is God-breathed (given by His inspiration) and profitable for instruction, for reproof and conviction of sin, for correction of error and discipline in obedience, [and] for training in righteousness (in holy living, in conformity to God's will in thought, purpose, and action)," (2 Timothy 3:16 AmpNT).

Revelation, Meaning, Comments, Examples, Supporting Scriptures:

"And we are setting these truths forth in words not taught by human wisdom but taught by the [Holy] Spirit, combining and interpreting spiritual truths with spiritual language [to those who possess the Holy Spirit]" (1 Corinthians 2:13 AmpNT).

The Word IS

God's Favor

"And now, brethren, I commend you to God, and to the word of his grace, which is able to build you up, and to give you an inheritance among all them which are sanctified" (Acts 20:32 KJV).
   "…and unto his word of favour…" (RhmNT).

God's Grace

"And now, brethren, I commend you to God, and to the word of his grace, which is able to build you up, and to give you an inheritance among all them which are sanctified" (Acts 20:32 KJV).

<u>Revelation, Meaning, Comments, Examples, Supporting Scriptures</u>:

Jesus is the Word of His grace who was given out of God's love for humanity. *"For God so loved the world, that he gave his only begotten Son, that whosoever believeth in him should not perish, but have everlasting life"* (John 3:16 KJV).

God's Judgments

"With my lips have I declared all the judgments of thy mouth" (Psalm 119:13 KJV).
   "I have talked forthrightly of all Your spoken judgments" (Har).

God's Law

"For a long while Israel was without the true God, without any priest who taught religion, without God's law" (2 Chronicles 15:3 Mof).

"But his delight is in the law of the Lord; and in his law doth he meditate day and night" (Psalm 1:2 KJV).

The Word IS

"Give ear, O my people, to my law: incline your ears to the words of my mouth" (Psalm 78:1 KJV).

"Open thou mine eyes, that I may behold wondrous things out of thy law" (Psalm 119:18 KJV).

"Remove from me the way of lying: and grant me thy law graciously" (Psalm 119:29 KJV).

"Give me understanding, and I shall keep thy law; yea, I shall observe it with my whole heart" (Psalm 119:34 KJV).

"So shall I keep thy law continually for ever and ever" (Psalm 119:44 KJV).

"The proud have had me greatly in derision: yet have I not declined from thy law" (Psalm 119:51 KJV).

"Horror hath taken hold upon me because of the wicked that forsake thy law" (Psalm 119:53 KJV).

"I have remembered thy name, O Lord, in the night, and have kept thy law" (Psalm 119:55 KJV).

"That this is a rebellious people, lying children, children that will not hear the law of the Lord:" (Isaiah 30:9 KJV).

Revelation, Meaning, Comments, Examples, Supporting Scriptures:

Our greatest pleasure must be in the Law of the Lord.

God's Power

"For our [preaching of the] glad tidings (the Gospel) came to you not only in word, but also in [its own inherent] power and in the Holy Spirit and with great conviction and absolute certainty [on our part]. You know what kind of men we proved [ourselves] to be among you for your good" (1 Thessalonians 1:5 AmpNT).

The Word IS

"...but as a message with power behind it—the effectual power, in fact, of the Holy Spirit..." (PhiNT).

"Who being the brightness of his glory, and the express image of his person, and upholding all things by the word of his power, when he had by himself purged our sins, sat down on the right hand of the Majesty on high:" (Hebrews 1:3 KJV).
"...Also bearing up all things by the utterance of his power..." (RhmNT).

Revelation, Meaning, Comments, Examples, Supporting Scriptures:

God's power is in the Word. That power is released when the Word is spoken. He opened His mouth and power manifested. What we see is the result of His word of power. (And God said, "Let there be...")

"For with God nothing is ever impossible and no word from God shall be without power or impossible of fulfillment" (Luke 1:37 AmpNT).

He put His power in a book, the Bible, and gave it to us. Therefore, we must know what it IS and what it DOES.

God's Testimonies

"I have rejoiced in the way of thy testimonies, as much as in all riches" (Psalm 119:14 KJV).

"Thy testimonies also are my delight and my counsellors" (Psalm 119:24 KJV).

"Quicken me after thy lovingkindness; so shall I keep the testimony of thy mouth" (Psalm 119:88 KJV).

Revelation, Meaning, Comments, Examples, Supporting Scriptures:

The Word is our advisor.

The Word IS

God's Way

"I have rejoiced in the way of thy testimonies, as much as in all riches" (Psalm 119:14 KJV).
> *"In the way of your decrees lies my joy, a joy beyond all wealth"* (Jerus).

"I will meditate in thy precepts, and have respect unto thy ways" (Psalm 119:15 KJV).

"Teach me, O Lord, the way of thy statutes; and I shall keep it unto the end" (Psalm 119:33 KJV).

"Turn away mine eyes from beholding vanity; and quicken thou me in thy way" (Psalm 119:37 KJV).
> *"turn away my eyes from all that is vile, grant me life by thy word"* (NEB).
> *"Turn away my eyes from beholding vanity (idols and idolatry); and restore me to vigorous life and health in Your ways"* (Amp).

<u>Revelation, Meaning, Comments, Examples, Supporting Scriptures</u>:

His way, His purpose and His path is His Word.

Good, Good News

"Then, said Hezekiah unto Isaiah, Good is the word of the Lord which thou hast spoken. And he said, Is it not good, if peace and truth be in my days?" (2 Kings 20:19 KJV).

"And the Lord answered the angel that talked with me with good words and comfortable words" (Zechariah 1:13 KJV).

"Then Phillip began, and taking this passage as his text, told him the Good News about Jesus" (Acts 8:35 TCNT).

"And have tasted the good word of God,..." (Hebrews 6:5 KJV).

The Word IS

"and have experienced how good God's message is…" (Wms).

"That word is the good news that has been brought to you" (1 Peter 1:25 Gspd).

Good Sense

"Keep therefore and do them; for this is your wisdom and your understanding in the sight of the nations, which shall hear all these statutes, and say, Surely this great nation is a wise and understanding people" (Deuteronomy 4:6 KJV).
   "…for so will your understanding and good sense be clear…" (Bas).

Gospel

"…preached the gospel of Jesus to him" (Acts 8:35 MofNT).

"In whom ye also trusted, after that ye heard the word of truth, the gospel of your salvation: in whom also after that ye believed, ye were sealed with that holy Spirit of promise," (Ephesians 1:13 KJV).

"And at the same time pray for us also, that God may open a door to us for the Word (the Gospel), to proclaim the mystery concerning Christ (the Messiah) on account of which I am in prison;" (Colossians 4:3 AmpNT).

"…And this word is nothing other than the Gospel which has been preached to you" (1 Peter 1:25 KnoxNT).

Gospel (The Good News)

"But the Word of the Lord (divine instruction, the Gospel) endures forever. And this Word is the good news which was preached to you" (1 Peter 1:25 AmpNT).
   "…And that is the word of the Gospel for you" (MofNT).
   "…And that is the Teaching of the Good News which has been told to you" (TCNT).

The Word IS

"...And this word is nothing other than the Gospel which has been preached to you" (KnoxNT).
"...That word is the good news that has been brought to you" (Gspd).

<u>Revelation, Meaning, Comments, Examples, Supporting Scriptures</u>:

"And Jesus went about all Galilee, teaching in their synagogues, and preaching the gospel of the kingdom, and healing all manner of sickness and all manner of disease among the people" (Matthew 4:23 KJV).
   "...proclaiming the Good News of the Kingdom..." (TCNT).
   "...preaching the gospel of the Reign..." (MofNT).
   "...announcing the good news of the kingdom..." (BerNT).

Gracious

"And the Lord answered gracious and comforting words to the angel who talked with me" (Zechariah 1:13 RSV).
   "And with that, the Lord answered him; gracious his words were, gracious and full of comfort" (Knox).

"And all bare him witness, and wondered at the gracious words which proceeded out of his mouth. And they said, Is not this Joseph's son?" (Luke 4:22 KJV).

"...and to his gracious word..." (Acts 20:32 KnoxNT).

Great Reward

"Moreover, by them is Your servant warned (reminded, illuminated, and instructed); and in keeping them there is great reward" (Psalm 19:11 Amp).

<u>Revelation, Meaning, Comments, Examples, Supporting Scriptures</u>:

Obedience to the Word results in great reward.

The Word IS

"…in following them there is rich profit" (Psalm 19:11 Mof).

Guide

"Your unchanging word is my delight, and the guide of my footsteps" (Psalm 119:24 Bas).

Hammer

"Is not My word like fire [that consumes all that cannot endure the test]? says the Lord, and like a hammer that breaks in pieces the rock [of most stubborn resistance]?" (Jeremiah 23:29 Amp).

Healing, Health

"My son, attend to my words; consent and submit to my sayings. Let them not depart from your sight; keep them in the center of your heart. For they are life to those who find them, healing and health to all their flesh" (Proverbs 4:20-22 Amp).
    "…to man's whole being they are health" (NAB).
    "…to those who find them, they are life, and health to all their being" (Mof).
    "…They are life to those who grasp them, health for the entire body" (Jerus).
    "…Keep these thoughts ever in mind; let them penetrate deep within your heart, for they will mean real life for you, and radiant health" (Tay).

"…and assents not to healthful words…" (1 Timothy 6:3 ABUV).

"Hold the pattern of healthful words…" (2 Timothy 1:13 ABUV).
    "An outline have thou of healthful discourses…" (RhmNT).

<u>Revelation, Meaning, Comments, Examples, Supporting Scriptures:</u>

We must grasp (take, receive) the Word for it to "be" health to us.

The Word IS

"If any man teach otherwise, and consent not to wholesome words, even the words of our Lord Jesus Christ, and to the doctrine which is according to godliness;" (1 Timothy 6:3 KJV).

Help

"Let me live that I may praise You, and let Your decrees help me" (Psalm 119:175 Amp).
    "...let thy decrees be my support" (NEB).
    "...So shall thy regulation help me" (Rhm).
    "...and may Your enactments uphold me" (Har).
    "...long be your rulings my help!" (Jerus).

Revelation, Meaning, Comments, Examples, Supporting Scriptures:

The Word is my support. The Word is called regulations, enactments, rulings, and decrees.

The Word is our help because Jesus is our help.

Heritage

"Your testimonies have I taken as a heritage forever, for they are the rejoicing of my heart" (Psalm 119:111 Amp).
    "Thy testimonies have I claimed as mine heritage for ever; and why? they are the very joy of my heart" (PBV).

Revelation, Meaning, Comments, Examples, Supporting Scriptures:

The Word has been given to me as a last Will and Testament, i.e. they are my heritage. The Testator, Jesus, died for me to inherit the Word of Life. I must claim my heritage to receive it. (See Hebrews 9:15-28 in several translations.)

Holy

"(Which he had promised afore by his prophets in the holy scriptures,)" (Romans 1:2 KJV).

The Word IS

"And that from a child thou hast known the holy scriptures, which are able to make thee wise unto salvation through faith which is in Christ Jesus" (2 Timothy 3:15 KJV).

Hope

"Remember the word unto thy servant, upon which thou hast caused me to hope" (Psalm 119:49 KJV).
   "Never forget your promises to me your servant; for they are my only hope" (Tay).

"They that fear thee will be glad when they see me; because I have hoped in thy word" (Psalm 119:74 KJV).

"Thou art my hiding place and my shield: I hope in thy word" (Psalm 119:114 KJV).

"I prevented the dawning of the morning, and cried: I hoped in thy word" (Psalm 119:147 KJV).
   "...I hope for the fulfillment of thy word" (NEB).

<u>Revelation, Meaning, Comments, Examples, Supporting Scriptures</u>:

Hope is trust. Hope is waiting with expectation. Hope is complete confidence. Hope encourages other believers. Jesus Christ, the Word, is our only hope.

"My eyes are straining to see your promises come true. When will you comfort me with your help?" (Psalm 119:82 Tay).

Human Being

"And the Word was made flesh, and dwelt among us, (and we beheld his glory, the glory as of the only begotten of the Father,) full of grace and truth" (John 1:14 KJV).
   "...became a human being..." (PhiNT).

The Word IS

<u>Revelation, Meaning, Comments, Examples, Supporting Scriptures</u>:

The Word, Jesus, is human and divine.

Instructions

"And these words, which I command thee this day, shall be in thine heart:" (Deuteronomy 6:6 KJV).
　"These instructions…are to be fixed in your mind" (AAT).

"On the second day, all the heads of fathers' houses, with the priests and Levites, gathered to Ezra the scribe to study and understand the words of divine instruction" (Nehemiah 8:13 Amp).

"For they are a rebellious people, lying sons, sons who will not hear the instruction of the Lord" (Isaiah 30:9 RSV).

"…and refuses his assent to sound instruction…" (1 Timothy 6:3 TCNT).

"As your example in wholesome instructions, keep before you…" (2 Timothy 1:13 Gspd).
　"Continue to be an example in wholesome instructions…" (Wms).

<u>Revelation, Meaning, Comments, Examples, Supporting Scriptures</u>:

The Word is instruction for the home (Deuteronomy 6:6-9), for leaders (Deuteronomy 17:18-20), for individuals, for all of life.

We are to put the Word on display.

"And these words, which I command thee this day, shall be in thine heart: And thou shalt teach them diligently unto thy children, and shalt talk of them when thou sittest in thine house, and when thou walkest by the way, and when thou liest down, and when thou risest up. And thou shalt bind them for a

The Word IS

sign upon thine hand, and they shall be as a frontlet between thine eyes. And thou shalt write them upon the posts of thy house, and on thy gates" (Deuteronomy 6:6-9 KJV).

"...whether you are busy or at rest..." (NAB).

(Deuteronomy 6:6-9 is also stated in Deuteronomy 11:18-21.)

"And it shall be, when he sitteth upon the throne of his kingdom, that he shall write him a copy of this law in a book out of that which is before the priests the Levites: And it shall be with him, and he shall read therein all the days of his life: that he may learn to fear the Lord his God, to keep all the words of this law and these statutes, to do them: That his heart be not lifted up above his brethren, and that he turn not aside from the commandment, to the right hand, or to the left: to the end that he may prolong his days in his kingdom, he, and his children, in the midst of Israel" (Deuteronomy 17:18-20 KJV).

Intelligence

"If you obey them they will give you a reputation for wisdom and intelligence..." (Deuteronomy 4:6 Tay).

Intelligible

"...The commandment of the Lord is intelligible, enlightening the mind" (Psalm 19:8 Har).

<u>Revelation, Meaning, Comments, Examples, Supporting Scriptures</u>:

Intelligible means understandable, capable of being understood. So, man is without excuse.

Joy

"Thy words were found, and I did eat them; and thy word was unto me the joy and rejoicing of mine heart: for I am called by thy name, O Lord God of hosts" (Jeremiah 15:16 KJV).

The Word IS

Just

"the Eternal's orders are just, a joy to the heart..." (Psalm 19:8 Mof).

Keener than the Sharpest Two-Edged Sword

"For the word of God is quick, and powerful, and sharper than any twoedged sword, piercing even to the dividing asunder of soul and spirit, and of the joints and marrow, and is a discerner of the thoughts and intents of the heart" (Hebrews 4:12 KJV).
> "...and is keener than the sharpest two-edged sword..." (Wey).

Kind

"...Surely his words are words of kindness for his people Israel?" (Micah 2:7 Jerus).

Knowledge

"For I have given unto them the words which thou gavest me; and they have received them, and have known surely that I came out from thee, and they have believed that thou didst send me" (John 17:8 KJV).
> "for I have given them the knowledge you bestowed on me..." (Rieu).

Lamp

"Thy word is a lamp unto my feet, and a light unto my path" (Psalm 119:105 KJV).

"...to which you will do well to pay attention (as if it were a lamp shining in a gloomy place), until the Day dawns and the Morning Star arises in your hearts:" (2 Peter 1:19 TCNT).
> "And we have the prophetic word [made] firmer still. You will do well to pay close attention to it as to a lamp shining in a dismal (squalid and dark) place, until the day breaks

The Word IS

through [the gloom] and the Morning Star rises (comes into being) in your hearts" (Amp).

Revelation, Meaning, Comments, Examples, Supporting Scriptures:

I see by the Word.

Lasting

"Being born again, not of corruptible seed, but of incorruptible, by the word of God, which liveth and abideth for ever" (1 Peter 1:23 KJV).
   "...the living, lasting word of God" (MofNT).

Revelation, Meaning, Comments, Examples, Supporting Scriptures:

We are born again in Jesus Christ who has overcome corruption.

Law

"And the Lord said unto Moses, Come up to me into the mount, and be there: and I will give thee tables of stone, and a law, and commandments which I have written; that thou mayest teach them" (Exodus 24:12 KJV).

"This book of the law shall not depart out of thy mouth; but thou shalt meditate therein day and night, that thou mayest observe to do according to all that is written therein: for then shalt thou make thy way prosperous, and then thou shalt have good success" (Joshua 1:8 KJV).

"And afterward he read all the words of the law, the blessings and cursings, according to all that is written in the book of the law" (Joshua 8:34 KJV).
   "...all else that the book of the law contains" (Knox).

The Word IS

"But be ye doers of the word, and not hearers only, deceiving your own selves. For if any be a hearer of the word, and not a doer, he is like unto a man beholding his natural face in a glass: For he beholdeth himself, and goeth his way, and straightway forgetteth what manner of man he was. But whoso looketh into the perfect law of liberty, and continueth therein, he being not a forgetful hearer, but a doer of the work, this man shall be blessed in his deed" (James 1:22-25 KJV).

<u>Revelation, Meaning, Comments, Examples, Supporting Scriptures</u>:

We are no longer under the law but under grace. Christ fulfilled the law.

Liberating

"And I will walk at liberty: for I seek thy precepts" (Psalm 119:45 KJV).

"But whoso looketh into the perfect law of liberty, and continueth therein, he being not a forgetful hearer, but a doer of the work, this man shall be blessed in his deed" (James 1:25 KJV).
 "...faultless law of freedom..." (MofNT).
 "...flawless law that makes men free..." (Gspd).

<u>Revelation, Meaning, Comments, Examples, Supporting Scriptures</u>:

We can walk at ease, in all freedom.

Life

"And he humbled thee, and suffered thee to hunger, and fed thee with manna, which thou knewest not, neither did thy fathers know; that he might make thee know that man doth not live by bread only, but by every word that proceedeth out of the mouth of the Lord doth man live" (Deuteronomy 8:3 KJV).

The Word IS

"This is my comfort in my suffering, That Thy word giveth me life" (Psalm 119:50 DeW).

"Uphold me according unto thy word, that I may live:…" (Psalm 119:116 KJV).

"Hear, O my son, and receive my sayings; and the years of thy life shall be many" (Proverbs 4:10 KJV).

"For they are life unto those that find them, and health to all their flesh" (Proverbs 4:22 KJV).
   "Keep these thoughts ever in mind; let them penetrate deep within your heart, for they will mean real life for you, and radiant health" (Tay).

"…he lives on every word that God utters" (Matthew 4:4 NEBNT).
   "…there is life for him in all the words which proceed from the mouth of God" (KnoxNT).

"And Jesus answered him, saying, It is written, That man shall not live by bread alone, but by every word of God" (Luke 4:4 KJV).

"It is the Spirit that quickeneth; the flesh profiteth nothing: the words that I speak unto you, they are spirit, and they are life" (John 6:63 KJV).

"Holding forth the word of life; that I may rejoice in the day of Christ, that I have not run in vain, neither labored in vain" (Philippians 2:16 KJV).

"[We are writing] about the Word of Life [in] Him Who existed from the beginning, Whom we have heard, Whom we have seen with our [own] eyes, Whom we have gazed upon [for ourselves] and have touched with our [own] hands" (1 John 1:1 AmpNT).
   *"Christ was alive when the world began, yet I myself have seen Him with my own eyes and listened to Him speak. I

The Word IS

have touched Him with my own hands. He is God's message of Life" (TayNT).
"...it is about the Word who is the Life that we are now writing" (TCNT).
"...it is the very message of life" (Gspd).
"...concerning the Word of life" (NASB).
"...it is concerning the Logos of Life that we are now writing" (Mon).

<u>Revelation, Meaning, Comments, Examples, Supporting Scriptures</u>:

The purpose for this work is because the Word is the message of Life.

Light

"Thy word is a lamp unto my feet, and a light unto my path" (Psalm 119:105 KJV).

"The entrance of thy words giveth light; it giveth understanding unto the simple" (Psalm 119:130 KJV).
  "When thy word goeth forth, it giveth light and understanding unto the simple" (PBV).
  "The unfolding of thy words gives light, Making the simple understand" (ABPS).
  "As your word unfolds, it gives light, and the simple understand" (Jerus).
  "Thy word is revealed, and all is light; it gives understanding even to the untaught" (NEB).

"For the commandment is a lamp; and the law is light; and reproofs of instruction are the way of life:" (Proverbs 6:23 KJV).

"For you are to them the light of life..." (Philippians 2:16 LamNT).

"We have also a more sure word of prophecy; whereunto ye do well that ye take heed, as unto a light that shineth in a dark

The Word IS

place, until the day dawn, and the day star arise in your hearts:" (2 Peter 1:19 KJV).

Living

"For the word of God is living, and active…" (Hebrews 4:12 ASV).
    "For the Logos of God is a living thing, active…" (MofNT).
    "For God's message is alive and full of power in action…" (Wms).
    "For the Word that God speaks is alive and active…" (PhiNT).
    "For whatever God says to us is full of living power…" (TayNT).

Lovable

"And I will delight myself in thy commandments, which I have loved. My hands also will I lift up unto thy commandments, which I have loved; and I will meditate in thy statutes" (Psalm 119:47-48 KJV).
    "Your commandments fill me with delight, I love them deeply…" (Jerus).

<u>Revelation, Meaning, Comments, Examples, Supporting Scriptures</u>:

We are to reverence the Word as we do the person of God, who is the Word.

Magnified

"I will worship toward thy holy temple, and praise thy name for thy loving-kindness and for thy truth: for thou hast magnified thy word above all thy name" (Psalm 138:2 KJV).

The Word IS

<u>Revelation, Meaning, Comments, Examples, Supporting Scriptures</u>:

"...for thou hast exalted above everything thy name and thy word" (Psalm 138:2 RSV).
   "...for you have made great above all things your name and your promise" (NAB).
   "...your promise is even greater than your fame" (Jerus).
   "...for your promises are backed by all the honor of your name" (Tay).

Meditation

"Princes also did sit and speak against me: but thy servant did meditate in thy statutes" (Psalm 119:23 KJV).

"Help me to discern the inner meaning of Your teachings, and I will meditate upon Your wonders" (Psalm 119:27 Har).

"My hands also will I lift up unto thy commandments, which I have loved; and I will meditate in thy statutes" (Psalm 119:48 KJV).

"O how love I thy law! it is my meditation all the day" (Psalm 119:97 KJV).

"I have more understanding than all my teachers: for thy testimonies are my meditation" (Psalm 119:99 KJV).

"Mine eyes prevent the night watches, that I might meditate in thy word" (Psalm 119:148 KJV).

Message of God

"...Come close, and listen to the message the Lord your God sends" (Joshua 3:9 Knox).

"And take the helmet of salvation, and the sword of the Spirit, which is the word of God:" (Ephesians 6:17 KJV).
   "...which is what God hath spoken:" (RhmNT).

The Word IS

"…which is the Message of God:" (TCNT).
"…which is the voice of God:" (Gspd).

Message of God's Love

"And now, brethren, I commend you to God, and to the word of his grace, which is able to build you up, and to give you an inheritance among all them which are sanctified" (Acts 20:32 KJV).
"…to the Message of His love…" (TCNT).

Message of Jesus Christ

"But what does it say? The Word (God's message in Christ) is near you, on your lips and in your heart; that is, the Word (the message, the basis and object) of faith which we preach," (Romans 10:8 AmpNT).

"So faith comes from hearing what is told, and that hearing comes through the message about Christ" (Romans 10:17 Gspd).
"…and what is heard comes by the preaching of Christ" (RSV).
"…and the message is the word of Christ" (PhiNT).
"…by the preaching [of the message that came from the lips] of Christ (the Messiah Himself)" (AmpNT).

<u>Revelation, Meaning, Comments, Examples, Supporting Scriptures</u>:

Jesus is a preacher. We must hear the message He preaches, which is the Word.

Mystery

"Withal praying also for us, that God would open unto us a door of utterance, to speak the mystery of Christ, for which I am also in bonds:" (Colossians 4:3 KJV).

The Word IS

<u>Revelation, Meaning, Comments, Examples, Supporting Scriptures:</u>

Mystery is:
- "...the sacred secret..." (Colossians 4:3 RhmNT).
- "...the open secret about Christ..." (Wms).
- "...the truths hidden in the Christ..." (TCNT).

Name of Jesus

"And he was clothed with a vesture dipped in blood: and his name is called The Word of God" (Revelation 19:13 KJV).
"...and the name by which he is called is The Word of God" (TCNT).

<u>Revelation, Meaning, Comments, Examples, Supporting Scriptures:</u>

When we speak the Word (the sword of the Spirit), we wield Jesus, the Word of God.

Near

"But the word is very nigh unto thee, in thy mouth, and in thy heart, that thou mayest do it" (Deuteronomy 30:14 KJV).
"...the word is very near you, it is on your lips and in your mind..." (Mof).
"...it is something very near to you, already in your mouths and in your hearts..." (NAB).
"...this message of mine is close to thy side; it rises to thy lips, it is printed on thy memory; thou hast only to fulfil it" (Knox).

Old

"I remembered thy judgments of old, O Lord; and have comforted myself" (Psalm 119:52 KJV).

"Concerning thy testimonies, I have known of old that thou hast founded them for ever" (Psalm 119:152 KJV).

The Word IS

<u>Revelation, Meaning, Comments, Examples, Supporting Scriptures</u>:

"I have long seen that thy decrees are valid for all time" (Psalm 119:152 Mof).

Operative

"For the Word that God speaks is alive and full of power [making it active, operative, energizing, and effective]; it is sharper than any two-edged sword, penetrating to the dividing line of the breath of life (soul) and [the immortal] spirit, and of joints and marrow [of the deepest parts of our nature], exposing and sifting and analyzing and judging the very thoughts and purposes of the heart" (Hebrews 4:12 AmpNT).

<u>Revelation, Meaning, Comments, Examples, Supporting Scriptures</u>:

The Word operates (works) in us.

Orders of God's Lips

"Nor have I strayed from the orders of His lips;…" (Job 23:12 Ber).

<u>Revelation, Meaning, Comments, Examples, Supporting Scriptures</u>:

The Word is from the mouth of God, written or proclaimed.

Path

"Make me to go in the path of thy commandments; for therein do I delight" (Psalm 119:35 KJV).

The Word IS

<u>Revelation, Meaning, Comments, Examples, Supporting Scriptures</u>:

"I have pondered on my behavior, and moved in the direction of Your commandments" (Psalm 119:59 Har).

Peace

"...What God is saying means peace for his people, for his friends, if only they renounce their folly" (Psalm 85:8 Jerus).

"Great peace have they which love thy law: and nothing shall offend them" (Psalm 119:165 KJV).
   "Peace is the reward of those who love thy law; no pitfalls beset their path" (NEB).

Penetrating

"For living is the word of God and energetic, And more cutting than any knife with two edges, And penetrating as far as a dividing asunder of soul and spirit,..." (Hebrews 4:12 Rhm).
   "...penetrating to the dividing line of the breath of life (soul) and [the immortal] spirit,..." (AmpNT).

<u>Revelation, Meaning, Comments, Examples, Supporting Scriptures</u>:

The Word goes deep.

Perfect

"The law of the Lord is perfect, converting the soul: the testimony of the Lord is sure, making wise the simple" (Psalm 19:7 KJV).

<u>Revelation, Meaning, Comments, Examples, Supporting Scriptures</u>:

The Word is flawless, it never fails.

The Word IS

Piercing

"For the word of God is quick, and powerful, and sharper than any twoedged sword, piercing even to the dividing asunder of soul and spirit, and of the joints and marrow, and is a discerner of the thoughts and intents of the heart" (Hebrews 4:12 KJV).

Pleasant

"O thou who art said to be the house of Jacob. Is the spirit of Yahweh impatient? Or are these his doings? Are not his words pleasant to him who is upright in his walk?" (Micah 2:7 Rhm).

"And Yahweh answered the messenger who was speaking to me in words that were pleasant, words that were consoling" (Zechariah 1:13 Rhm).

Pleasure

"but finds his pleasure in the law of Yahweh…" (Psalm 1:2 Jerus).
    "But whose greatest pleasure is in the law of the Lord…" (Har).

Revelation, Meaning, Comments, Examples, Supporting Scriptures:

"A word fitly spoken and in due season is like apples of gold in settings of silver" (Proverbs 25:11 Amp).

Think on what a pleasure that is.

Powerful

"For no word of God shall be void of power" (Luke 1:37 ASV).
    "Because no word of God shall be without power" (ABUV).
    "For with God nothing is ever impossible and no word from God shall be without power or impossible of fulfillment" (AmpNT).

The Word IS

"For the word of God is quick, and powerful, and sharper than any twoedged sword, piercing even to the dividing asunder of soul and spirit, and of the joints and marrow, and is a discerner of the thoughts and intents of the heart" (Hebrews 4:12 KJV).

Prevention from Sin

"Thy word have I hid in mine heart, that I might not sin against thee" (Psalm 119:11 KJV).

"I have refrained my feet from every evil way, that I might keep thy word" (Psalm 119:101 KJV).
> *"I have restrained my feet from every evil way, that I might keep Your word [hearing, receiving, loving, and obeying it]"* (Amp).

<u>Revelation, Meaning, Comments, Examples, Supporting Scriptures:</u>

Hiding the Word in my heart is treasuring the Word. There is purpose in treasuring the Word; to avoid sin.

Withdraw, run, retreat from sin; turn away from it.

Profitable

"All scripture is given by inspiration of God, and is profitable for doctrine, for reproof, for correction, for instruction in righteousness:" (2 Timothy 3:16 KJV).

<u>Revelation, Meaning, Comments, Examples, Supporting Scriptures:</u>

The Word is profitable, but we are not to corrupt the Word of God for profit. The Word increases us when we read, meditate and obey it. There is a difference in profiting from the Word and making a profit from the Word.

"For we are not, as the many, driving a petty trade with the word of God…" (2 Corinthians 2:17 Rhm).

The Word IS

"For I seek not profit (like most) by setting the word of God to sale..." (Con).

"Unlike many people, we are not in the habit of making profit out of God's Message..." (TCNT).

"Unlike most teachers, we do not adulterate God's word..." (Wey).

"For I am no peddler of God's message, like most men..." (Gspd).

"For I am not like most, trafficking in the word of God..." (Mon).

"For we are not like the great number who make use of the word of God for profit..." (BasNT).

"For we do not, like so many, peddle an adulterated message of God..." (BerNT).

"At least we don't peddle an impure Word of God like many others..." (Beck).

Prophecy

"Turn back, when the time comes, to this record of divine prophecy, and read it afresh; you shall learn, then, that none of these signs are lacking, none waited for the coming of the next" (Isaiah 34:16 Knox).

"But is now disclosed and through the prophetic Scriptures is made known to all nations, according to the command of the eternal God, [to win them] to obedience to the faith," (Romans 16:26 AmpNT).

"We have also a more sure word of prophecy; whereunto ye do well that ye take heed, as unto a light that shineth in a dark place, until the day dawn, and the day star arise in your hearts:" (2 Peter 1:19 KJV).

"Blessed is he that readeth, and they that hear the words of this prophecy, and keep those things which are written therein: for the time is at hand" (Revelation 1:3 KJV).

"For I testify unto every man that heareth the words of the prophecy of this book, If any man shall add unto these things,

The Word IS

God shall add unto him the plagues that are written in this book: And if any man shall take away from the words of the book of this prophecy, God shall take away his part out of the book of life, and out of the holy city, and from the things which are written in this book" (Revelation 22:18-19 KJV).

Revelation, Meaning, Comments, Examples, Supporting Scriptures:

Prophecy is the Word from God spoken through men who are influenced, moved, carried away, and impelled by the Holy Spirit (read 2 Peter 1:20-21). The Word is more sure than anything spoken by men.

"For I delivered unto you first of all that which I also received, how that Christ died for our sins according to the scriptures;" (1 Corinthians 15:3 KJV).

Pure

"...the word of Yahweh is without dross..." (2 Samuel 22:31 Jerus).

"The words and promises of the Lord are pure words, like silver refined in an earthen furnace, purified seven times over" (Psalm 12:6 Amp).
   "The Words of Yahweh are without alloy, nature's silver coming from the earth seven times refined" (Jerus).
   "The promises of the Lord are promises that are pure, silver refined in a furnace on the ground, purified seven times" (RSV).
   "The sayings of Jehovah are pure sayings; Silver tried in a furnace of earth, Seven times refined" (ABPS).

"Thy word is very pure: therefore thy servant loveth it" (Psalm 119:140 KJV).

"Every word of God is tried and purified; He is a shield to those who trust and take refuge in Him" (Proverbs 30:5 Amp).

The Word IS

<u>Revelation, Meaning, Comments, Examples, Supporting Scriptures</u>:

We want what is pure: genuine, the real deal. The Word is refined, trusted and tested, tried to the utmost, thoroughly tested, well tried.

"The fear of the Lord is clean, enduring for ever: the judgments of the Lord are true and righteous altogether" (Psalm 19:9 KJV).

Quick

"For the word of God is quick, and powerful, and sharper than any twoedged sword, piercing even to the dividing asunder of soul and spirit, and of the joints and marrow, and is a discerner of the thoughts and intents of the heart" (Hebrews 4:12 KJV).

Reliable

"...The decrees of the Lord are reliable" (Psalm 19:7 Har).

"For the promises of the Lord are reliable, and all that He does is trustworthy" (Psalm 33:4 Har).

<u>Revelation, Meaning, Comments, Examples, Supporting Scriptures</u>:

The Word never fails. It can be counted on.

Revelation of God's Grace

"And now, brethren, I commend you to God, and to the word of his grace, which is able to build you up, and to give you an inheritance among all them which are sanctified" (Acts 20:32 KJV).
   "...and to the revelation of his grace..." (Rieu).

The Word IS

Reviver

"I am completely discouraged—I lie in the dust. Revive me by your Word" (Psalm 119:25 Tay).

"Turn away my eyes from looking at futilities, and revive me in Thy ways" (Psalm 119:37 Ber).
    "Turn away my eyes from beholding vanity (idols and idolatry); and restore me to vigorous life and health in Your ways" (Amp).

"Lo, I have longed for thy precepts; Revive me through thy righteousness" (Psalm 119:40 AAT).

"According to thy mercy revive me. And I will keep the testimony of thy mouth" (Psalm 119:88 ABPS).

"O Jehovah, according to thy judgments revive me" (Psalm 119:149 ABPS).

"Plead my cause and redeem me; revive me and give me life according to Your word" (Psalm 119:154 Amp).

"Great are thy tender mercies, O Lord: quicken me according to thy judgments" (Psalm 119:156 KJV).

"Consider how I love Your precepts; revive me and give life to me, O Lord, according to Your loving-kindness!" (Psalm 119:159 Amp).
    "...O Jehovah, according to thy mercy revive me..." (ABPS).

<u>Revelation, Meaning, Comments, Examples, Supporting Scriptures</u>:

Because He loves us, He keeps us alive.

Life is God's choice.

The Word gives me life.

The Word IS

Right

"The statutes of the Lord are right, rejoicing the heart: the commandment of the Lord is pure, enlightening the eyes" (Psalm 19:8 KJV).

"The precepts of the Lord are right, rejoicing the heart; the commandment of the Lord is pure and bright, enlightening the eyes" (Amp).

"For the word of the Lord is right; and all his works are done in truth" (Psalm 33:4 KJV).

"For the word of Jehovah is right; And all his work is done in faithfulness" (ASV).

Righteous Altogether

"The fear of the Lord is clean, enduring for ever: the judgments of the Lord are true and righteous altogether" (Psalm 19:9 KJV).

Righteous, Right, Upright

"And what nation is there so great, that hath statutes and judgments so righteous as all this law, which I set before you this day?" (Deuteronomy 4:8 KJV).

"Behold, I have longed after thy precepts: quicken me in thy righteousness" (Psalm 119:40 KJV).

"At midnight I will rise to give thanks unto thee because of thy righteous judgments" (Psalm 119:62 KJV).

"I know, O Lord, that Your judgments are right and righteous, and that in faithfulness You have afflicted me" (Psalm 119:75 Amp).

"Mine eyes fail for thy salvation, and for the word of thy righteousness" (Psalm 119:123 KJV).

The Word IS

"Therefore I esteem all thy precepts concerning all things to be right; and I hate every false way" (Psalm 119:128 KJV).
   "Therefore I esteem as right all, yes, all Your precepts; I hate every false way" (AMP).

"Righteous art thou, O Lord, and upright are thy judgments" (Psalm 119:137 KJV).

"Thy testimonies are righteous for ever..." (Psalm 119:144 RSV).
   "Your laws are always fair..." (Tay).

"Thy word is true from the beginning: and every one of thy righteous judgments endureth for ever" (Psalm 119:160 KJV).
   "...and your upright decision is unchanging for ever" (Bas).

"Seven times a day do I praise thee because of thy righteous judgments" (Psalm 119:164 KJV).

"My tongue shall speak of thy word: for all thy commandments are righteousness" (Psalm 119:172 KJV).

Sacred

"Which He promised in advance [long ago] through His prophets in the sacred Scriptures" (Romans 1:2 AmpNT).

"and that from a babe thou hast known the sacred writings,..." (2 Timothy 3:15 ASV).

Salvation

"Let thy mercies come also unto me, O Lord, even thy salvation, according to thy word" (Psalm 119:41 KJV).

"Men and brethren, children of the stock of Abraham, and whosoever among you feareth God, to you is the word of this salvation sent" (Acts 13:26 KJV).
   "...it was to us that the Message of this Salvation was sent" (TCNT).

The Word IS

"Wherefore lay apart all filthiness and superfluity of naughtiness, and receive with meekness the engrafted word, which is able to save your souls" (James 1:21 KJV).

Revelation, Meaning, Comments, Examples, Supporting Scriptures:

According to John 3:16, Jesus is our Savior and He is love. He is the Word. *"…and the Word was God"* (John 1:1 KJV).

The Word is our Savior.

Sayings of God's Mouth

"…Above my allotted portion have I laid up the sayings of His mouth" (Job 23:12 YLT).
   "…I have esteemed the words of his mouth more than my necessary food" (KJV).

"When therefore he was risen from the dead, his disciples remembered that he had said this unto them: and they believed the scripture, and the word which Jesus had said" (John 2:22 KJV).

Revelation, Meaning, Comments, Examples, Supporting Scriptures:

The Word is from the mouth of God, written or proclaimed.

Scroll

"…this scroll of the law…" (Deuteronomy 31:26 Rhm).

"This scroll of the law must not cease…" (Joshua 1:8 Rhm).

Seed

"What the sower sows is the word" (Mark 4:14 Wey).
   "What the sower sows is the message" (Gspd).

The Word IS

"Now the parable is this: The seed is the word of God" (Luke 8:11 KJV).

Revelation, Meaning, Comments, Examples, Supporting Scriptures:

We must sow the seed, the Word, to get a harvest and we must sow for a specific harvest; the Word on health to be healthy, the Word on prosperity to be prosperous, because it produces after its kind. (See Matthew 13:3-32, Mark 4:3-32, Luke 8:4-15)

Settled in Heaven

"For ever, O Lord, thy word is settled in heaven" (Psalm 119:89 KJV).

Sharper than Any Two-Edged Sword

"For the word of God is quick, and powerful, and sharper than any twoedged sword, piercing even to the dividing asunder of soul and spirit, and of the joints and marrow, and is a discerner of the thoughts and intents of the heart" (Hebrews 4:12 KJV).

Sincere

"The speech of the Lord is sincere…" (Psalm 18:30 AAT).

Sound Doctrine

"…and refuses his assent to sound instruction…" (1 Timothy 6:3 TCNT).

"Hold fast the form of sound words, which thou hast heard of me, in faith and love which is in Christ Jesus" (2 Timothy 1:13 KJV).

"Holding fast the faithful word as he hath been taught, that he may be able by sound doctrine both to exhort and to convince the gainsayers" (Titus 1:9 KJV).

The Word IS

Spirit

"It is the Spirit that quickeneth; the flesh profiteth nothing: the words that I speak unto you, they are spirit, and they are life" (John 6:63 KJV).
  "...The messages I bring you are spirit and life" (BerNT).

Spiritual Law

"Who also hath made us able ministers of the new testament; not of the letter, but of the spirit: for the letter killeth, but the spirit giveth life" (2 Corinthians 3:6 KJV).
  "...It is a spiritual, not a written law..." (KnoxNT).

Steadfast

"They are steadfast always and for ever, They are made in truth and uprightness" (Psalm 111:8 DeW).

Strength

"My soul melteth for heaviness: strengthen thou me according unto thy word" (Psalm 119:28 KJV).
  "My life dissolves and weeps itself away for heaviness; raise me up and strengthen me according to [the promises of] Your word" (Amp).

Sure

"The promises of the Lord are sure, like tried silver, freed from dross, sevenfold refined" (Psalm 12:6 NAB).

"The law of the Lord is perfect, converting the soul: the testimony of the Lord is sure, making wise the simple" (Psalm 19:7 KJV).

"Thy testimonies are very sure: holiness becometh thine house, O Lord, for ever" (Psalm 93:5 KJV).

The Word IS

"The works of his hands are verity and judgment; all his commandments are sure" (Psalm 111:7 KJV).

"The works of His hands are [absolute] truth and justice [faithful and right]; and all His decrees and precepts are sure (fixed, established, and trustworthy)" (Amp).

"And we have the prophetic word made more sure..." (2 Peter 1:19 RSV).

<u>Revelation, Meaning, Comments, Examples, Supporting Scriptures</u>:

The Word is not going to move. It's not going to change. It cannot change. It is reliable according to:

"For I am the Lord: I will speak, and the word that I shall speak shall come to pass; it shall be no more prolonged: for in your days, O rebellious house, will I say the word, and will perform it, saith the Lord God. Again the word of the Lord came to me, saying, Son of man, behold, they of the house of Israel say, The vision that he seeth is for many days to come, and he prophesieth of the times that are far off. Therefore say unto them, Thus saith the Lord God; There shall none of my words be prolonged any more, but the word which I have spoken shall be done, saith the Lord God" (Ezekiel 12:25-28 KJV).

Sweet

"More to be desired are they than gold, even than much fine gold; they are sweeter also than honey and drippings from the honeycomb" (Psalm 19:10 Amp).

"How sweet are Your words to my taste, Sweeter than honey to my mouth!" (Psalm 119:103 NKJV).

"And have tasted God's utterance to be sweet..." (Hebrews 6:5 RhmNT).

The Word IS

Sweeter than Honey and the Honey Comb

"How sweet are Your words to my taste, Sweeter than honey to my mouth!" (Psalm 119:103 NKJV).

"And he said unto me, Son of man, cause thy belly to eat, and fill thy bowels with this roll that I give thee. Then did I eat it; and it was in my mouth as honey for sweetness" (Ezekiel 3:3 KJV).

<u>Revelation, Meaning, Comments, Examples, Supporting Scriptures</u>:

The Word is "better than" anything we can compare it to. We should desire the "better than" who is God, the Word.

Sword, Sword of the Spirit

"And take the helmet of salvation, and the sword of the Spirit, which is the word of God:" (Ephesians 6:17 KJV).

Teaching

"…he shall have a copy of this Teaching written for him by the Levitical priests" (Deuteronomy 17:18 Tor).

"…you shall read this Teaching aloud in the presence of…" (Deuteronomy 31:11 Tor).

"Welcome the teaching from his lips…" (Job 22:22 Jerus).

"Give ear, O my people, to my teaching…" (Psalm 78:1 RSV).

"Let Christ's teaching live in your hearts, making you rich in the true wisdom…" (Colossians 3:16 PhiNT).
   "Remember what Christ taught and let His words enrich your lives and make you wise…" (TayNT).

"…able both to exhort in the healthful teaching…" (Titus 1:9 ABV).

The Word IS

"...competent to encourage others with wholesome teaching..." (Wms).

"...able to give comfort by right teaching..." (BasNT).

Terms of Deliverance

"Receive, I pray thee, from his mouth, the terms of deliverance..." (Job:22:22 Sept).

Tried, Tested

"As for God, his way is perfect; the word of the Lord is tried: he is a buckler to all them that trust in him" (2 Samuel 22:31 KJV).

"The words of the Lord are pure words: as silver tried in a furnace of earth, purified seven times" (Psalm 12:6 KJV).

"As for God, his way is perfect: the word of the Lord is tried: he is a buckler to all those that trust in him" (Psalm 18:30 KJV).
   "Such is my God, unsullied in his dealings; his promises are like metal tested in the fire..." (Knox).

"Every word of God is tried and purified; He is a shield to those who trust and take refuge in Him" (Proverbs 30:5 Amp).

True, Truth

"And now, O Lord God, thou art that God, and thy words be true, and thou hast promised this goodness unto thy servant:" (2 Samuel 7:28 KJV).

"The teachings of the Lord are true, making one happy..." (Psalm 19:8 Har).

"The fear of the Lord is clean, enduring for ever: the judgments of the Lord are true and righteous altogether" (Psalm 19:9 KJV).

"The word of the Lord holds true, and all his work endures" (Psalm 33:4 NEB).

The Word IS

"I have chosen the way of truth: thy judgments have I laid before me" (Psalm 119:30 KJV).

"And take not the word of truth utterly out of my mouth; for I have hoped in thy judgments" (Psalm 119:43 KJV).

"Thy righteousness is an everlasting righteousness, and thy law is the truth" (Psalm 119:142 KJV).

"Thou art near, O Lord; and all thy commandments are truth" (Psalm 119:151 KJV).

"Thy word is true from the beginning: and every one of thy righteous judgments endureth for ever" (Psalm 119:160 KJV).
    "Your sayings are supremely true:…" (Har).
    "The sum of thy word is truth:…" (Rhm).

"But I will shew thee that which is noted in the scripture of truth:…" (Daniel 10:21 KJV).

"Sanctify them through thy truth: thy word is truth" (John 17:17 KJV).
    "Consecrate them in the truth:…" (Rieu).
    "make them holy by the truth:…" (Phi).
    "…thy Message is Truth" (TCNT).
    "Sanctify them [purify, consecrate, separate them for Yourself, make them holy] by the Truth; Your Word is Truth" (Amp).

"By [speaking] the word of truth, in the power of God, with the weapons of righteousness for the right hand [to attack] and for the left hand [to defend];" (2 Corinthians 6:7 Amp).
    "…speaking the word of truth, working with the power of God, fighting with the weapons of righteousness, both for attack and for defense," (Con).
    "…speaking the plain truth, and living by the power of God. Our sole defense, our only weapon is a life of integrity," (Phi).
    "We must rely on the truth of the Word…" (Nor).

The Word IS

"In whom ye also trusted, after that ye heard the word of truth, the gospel of your salvation: in whom also after that ye believed, ye were sealed with that holy Spirit of promise," (Ephesians 1:13 KJV).

"For this cause also thank we God without ceasing, because, when ye received the word of God which ye heard of us, ye received it not as the word of men, but as it is in truth, the word of God, which effectually worketh also in you that believe" (1 Thessalonians 2:13 KJV).

"Study to shew thyself approved unto God, a workman that needeth not to be ashamed, rightly dividing the word of truth" (2 Timothy 2:15 KJV).

"Of his own will begat he us with the word of truth, that we should be a kind of firstfruits of his creatures" (James 1:18 KJV).

<u>Revelation, Meaning, Comments, Examples, Supporting Scriptures</u>:

"Then said Jesus to those Jews which believed on him, If ye continue in my word, then are ye my disciples indeed; And ye shall know the truth, and the truth shall make you free" (John 8:31-32 KJV).

Continuing in the Word reveals the truth and that truth makes you free (see John 8:32).

Let God be true and every man a lie.

Trustworthy

"...The decree of the Lord is trustworthy,..." (Psalm 19:7 AAT).

"Thy testimonies are so trustworthy;..." (Psalm 93:5 Ber).

"The works of his hands are faithful and just; all his precepts are trustworthy" (Psalm 111:7 RSV).

The Word IS

"So shall I have wherewith to answer him that reproacheth me: for I trust in thy word" (Psalm 119:42 KJV).

Undefiled

"The law of the Lord is an undefiled law…" (Psalm 19:7 PBV).

Understanding

"Keep therefore and do them; for this is your wisdom and your understanding in the sight of the nations which shall hear all these statutes and say, Surely this great nation is a wise and understanding people" (Deuteronomy 4:6 KJV).

"I have more understanding than all my teachers: for thy testimonies are my meditation. I understand more than the ancients, because I keep thy precepts" (Psalm 119:99-100 KJV).

"Your precepts endow me with perception;…" (Psalm 119:104 Jerus).

"The entrance of thy words giveth light; it giveth understanding unto the simple" (Psalm 119:130 KJV).

"Let my cry come near before thee, O Lord: give me understanding according to thy word" (Psalm 119:169 KJV).
   "…give me the common sense you promised" (Tay).

Upright

"…the Eternal's rulings are upright, and altogether just" (Psalm 19:9 Mof).

"They are steadfast always and for ever. They are made in truth and uprightness" (Psalm 111:8 DeW).

The Word IS

Useful

"All Scripture is divinely inspired, and useful..." (2 Timothy 3:16 Gspd).

Revelation, Meaning, Comments, Examples, Supporting Scriptures:

The Word is practical; it is applicable to every area of our lives. It is not abstract.

Voice of God

"And take the helmet of salvation, and the sword of the Spirit, which is the word of God:" (Ephesians 6:17 KJV).
   "...which is the voice of God" (Gspd).

Revelation, Meaning, Comments, Examples, Supporting Scriptures:

When we hear the Word, we are hearing the very voice of God. When God, by the Holy Spirit, brings a scripture to our remembrance, He is speaking to us. We are hearing His voice.

What God Has Spoken

"And take the helmet of salvation, and the sword of the Spirit, which is the word of God:" (Ephesians 6:17 KJV).
   "...which is what God hath spoken:" (Rhm).

Wholesome

"If any man teach otherwise, and consent not to wholesome words, even the words of our Lord Jesus Christ, and to the doctrine which is according to godliness;" (1 Timothy 6:3 KJV).
   "But if anyone teaches otherwise and does not assent to the sound and wholesome messages of our Lord Jesus Christ (the Messiah) and the teaching which is in agreement with godliness (piety toward God)," (Amp).

The Word IS

"Hold fast the form of sound words,…" (2 Timothy 1:13 KJV).
   "As your example in wholesome instructions, keep before you…" (Gspd).
   "Continue to be an example in wholesome instructions…" (Wms).

"who have known the wholesome nourishment of the Word of God…" (Hebrews 6:5 Phi).

Wisdom

"Keep therefore and do them; for this is your wisdom and your understanding in the sight of the nations which shall hear all these statutes and say, Surely this great nation is a wise and understanding people" (Deuteronomy 4:6 KJV).

"Thou through thy commandments hast made me wiser than mine enemies: for they are ever with me" (Psalm 119:98 KJV).

Revelation, Meaning, Comments, Examples, Supporting Scriptures:

The Word is my constant guide.

Witness Against You

"Take this book of the law, and put it in the side of the ark of the covenant of the Lord your God, that it may be there for a witness against thee" (Deuteronomy 31:26 KJV).

Wondrous, Wonder, Wonderful

"Open thou mine eyes, that I may behold wondrous things out of thy law" (Psalm 119:18 KJV).

"Thy testimonies are wonderful: therefore doth my soul keep them" (Psalm 119:129 KJV).
   "Your testimonies are wonderful [far exceeding anything conceived by man]; therefore my [penitent] self keeps them [hearing, receiving, loving, and obeying them]" (Amp).

The Word IS

<u>Revelation, Meaning, Comments, Examples, Supporting Scriptures:</u>

The wonders of the Word are revealed to us:

"Unveil thou mine eyes that I may discern wondrous things out of thy law" (Psalm 119:18 Rhm).
　"Give me discernment, that I may notice wonderful things in Your law" (Har).
　"Take the veil from my eyes, that I may see the marvels that spring from thy law" (NEB).

Why would you not want what is wonderful?

Word of Christ, Word of the Lord, Word of God

"Let the word of Christ dwell in you richly in all wisdom; teaching and admonishing one another in psalms and hymns and spiritual songs, singing with grace in your hearts to the Lord" (Colossians 3:16 KJV).

"For from you sounded out the word of the Lord not only in Macedonia and Achaia, but also in every place your faith to God-ward is spread abroad; so that we need not to speak any thing" (1 Thessalonians 1:8 KJV).
　"And now the Word of the Lord has spread out from you..." (Tay).

"For this cause also thank we God without ceasing, because, when ye received the word of God which ye heard of us, ye received it not as the word of men, but as it is in truth, the word of God, which effectually worketh also in you that believe" (1 Thessalonians 2:13 KJV).

"If any man teach otherwise, and consent not to wholesome words, even the words of our Lord Jesus Christ, and to the doctrine which is according to godliness;" (1 Timothy 6:3 KJV).

"Wherein I suffer trouble, as an evil doer, even unto bonds; but the word of God is not bound" (2 Timothy 2:9 KJV).

The Word IS

"...But the Message of God is not fettered" (TCNT).
"...(But there is no prison for the word of God)" (Gspd).
"...but the word of God is not shackled" (Ber).
"...yet the word of God is not chained" (Wey).

"This then is the message which we have heard of him, and declare unto you, that God is light, and in him is no darkness at all" (1 John 1:5 KJV).

<u>Revelation, Meaning, Comments, Examples, Supporting Scriptures</u>:

For more evidence see Exodus 24:4,12, 25:21, 31:18, 32:16, 34:27, 34:32; Leviticus 26:46.

Writing of God

"And the tables were the work of God, and the writing was the writing of God, graven upon the tables" (Exodus 32:16 KJV).
    "...and the engraving the engraving of God..." (Sprl).
    "...having inscriptions...by God himself..." (NAB).
    "...a divine hand had traced the characters..." (Knox).
    "...inscribed on the tablets" (Mof).
    "...incised..." (Tor).
    "...cut on the stones" (Bas).

<u>Revelation, Meaning, Comments, Examples, Supporting Scriptures</u>:

God wrote the Word! He not only penned the commandments on tables, He wrote the Word, by inspiration, on the mind and hearts of men who recorded what He said on paper.

"Every Scripture is God-breathed (given by His inspiration) and profitable for instruction, for reproof and conviction of sin, for correction of error and discipline in obedience, [and] for training in righteousness (in holy living, in conformity to God's will in thought, purpose, and action)," (2 Timothy 3:16 Amp).

The Word DOES

Accomplishes God's Will and Purpose

"Seek ye out of the book of the Lord, and read: no one of these shall fail, none shall want her mate: for my mouth it hath commanded, and his spirit it hath gathered them" (Isaiah 34:16 KJV).

"So shall my word be that goeth forth out of my mouth: it shall not return unto me void, but it shall accomplish that which I please, and it shall prosper in the things whereto I sent it" (Isaiah 55:11 KJV).

> *"...so the word that goes from my mouth does not return to me empty, without carrying out my will and succeeding in what it was sent to do"* (Jerus).
>
> *"...so shall my word be that goes forth from my mouth; It shall not return to me void, but shall do my will, achieving the end for which I sent it"* (NAB).
>
> *"...so with the promise that has passed my lips; it falls not fruitless and in vain, but works out what I will, and carried out my purpose"* (Mof).

<u>Revelation, Meaning, Comments, Examples, Supporting Scriptures</u>:

Jesus speaks the Word; the Word works because it is the Word of His power (Hebrews 1:3). Reinhard Bonnke said God told him, "My Word in your mouth is just as powerful as My Word in my mouth."

No Word of God shall fail; it will find fulfillment, i.e. its mate. Fulfillment is the mate of the promise. The promise becomes reality.

Adds Life, Prosperity, Peace

"...What God is saying means peace for his people, for his friends, if only they renounce their folly" (Psalm 85:8 Jerus).

The Word DOES

"My son, forget not my law; but let thine heart keep my commandments; For length of days, and long life, and peace, shall they add to thee" (Proverbs 3:1-2 KJV).

> *"My son, forget not my law or teaching, but let your heart keep my commandments; For length of days and years of a life [worth living] and tranquility [inward and outward and continuing through old age till death], these shall they add to you"* (Amp).
>
> *"My son, do not forget my teaching, but keep my commands in your heart, for they will prolong your life many years and bring you prosperity"* (NIV).
>
> *"My son, do not forget my teaching, But let your heart keep my commandments; For length of days and years of life And peace they will add to you"* (NASB).

Admonishes

"Now all these things happened unto them for ensamples: and they are written for our admonition, upon whom the ends of the world are come" (1 Corinthians 10:11 KJV).

Answers Our Requests

"If ye abide in me, and my words abide in you, ye shall ask what ye will, and it shall be done unto you" (John 15:7 KJV).

> *"If you remain in union with me and my words remain in you, you may ask whatever you please and you shall have it"* (Wms).

<u>Revelation, Meaning, Comments, Examples, Supporting Scriptures:</u>

The Word must abide in us. We must stay in the Word.

"And this is the confidence that we have in him, that, if we ask any thing according to his will, he heareth us: And if we know that he hear us, whatsoever we ask, we know that we have the petitions that we desired of him" (1 John 5:14-15 KJV).

The Word DOES

Benefits

"...Do not my words benefit him who walks honestly?" (Micah 2:7 Ber).

Brings Joy

"Your words are what sustained me; they are food to my hungry soul. They bring joy to my sorrowing heart and delight to me. How proud I am to bear Your name, O Lord" (Jeremiah 15:16 Tay).

Builds Up Character

"...a Message which has the power to build up your character..." (Acts 20:32 TCNT).

Builds You Up

"And now, brethren, I commend you to God, and to the word of his grace, which is able to build you up, and to give you an inheritance among all them which are sanctified" (Acts 20:32 KJV).

Revelation, Meaning, Comments, Examples, Supporting Scriptures:

Jesus is the Word who accomplishes all the Word does.

Causes One to Believe Jesus is the Christ, the Son of God

"And many other signs truly did Jesus in the presence of his disciples, which are not written in this book: But these are written, that ye might believe that Jesus is the Christ, the Son of God; and that believing ye might have life through his name" (John 20:30-31 KJV).

> "His disciples saw Jesus do many other miracles that are not written in this book:...so that you believe Jesus is the promised Savior..." (Beck).

The Word DOES

Causes One to Do No Iniquity and to Do No Unrighteousness

"Blessed are they that keep his testimonies, and that seek him with the whole heart. They also do no iniquity: they walk in his ways" (Psalm 119:2-3 KJV).
    "...Yes, they do no unrighteousness [no willful wandering from His precepts]; they walk in His ways" (Amp).

<u>Revelation, Meaning, Comments, Examples, Supporting Scriptures</u>:

The Word causes me not to sin, but to obey God.

Cautions

"...and were recorded to serve as a caution to us..." (1 Corinthians 10:11 TCNT).

Cleanses

"Wherewithal shall a young man cleanse his way? by taking heed thereto according to thy word" (Psalm 119:9 KJV).
    "Wherewithal shall a young man cleanse his way? even by ruling himself after thy word" (PBV).
    "How can a youth remain pure? By behaving as your word prescribes" (Jerus).
    "How can a young man keep life clean? By keeping to thy word" (Mof).

"Now ye are clean through the word which I have spoken unto you" (John 15:3 KJV).
    "You are already cleansed by means of the Word..." (Nor).
    "You are cleansed and pruned already, because of the word which I have given you [the teachings I have discussed with you]" (Amp).

"That he might sanctify and cleanse it with the washing of water by the word," (Ephesians 5:26 KJV).
    "...sanctify it, having cleansed it" (ASV).

The Word DOES

"...to consecrate her, after cleansing her with the bath in water through her confession of him" (Gspd).
"To make her holy and clean washed by baptism and God's word," (Tay).

<u>Revelation, Meaning, Comments, Examples, Supporting Scriptures:</u>

The Word is revelation and demonstration of how to live.

The Word is the rule of life (see Deuteronomy 27:26 Amp).

We are to live by the Word (see Psalm 119:9):
- Ruling ourselves after the Word (PBV).
- Guarding it according to thy Word (RSV).
- Conforming my life to God's Word (Amp).
- Living a clean life only by paying attention to what God says (Har).
- Behaving as the Word prescribes (Jerus).

Comforts and Consoles

"Wherefore comfort one another with these words" (1 Thessalonians 4:18 KJV).
 "So then be consoling one another with these words" (Rhm).

Conforms Your Life

"How shall a young man cleanse his way? By taking heed and keeping watch [on himself] according to Your word [conforming his life to it]" (Psalm 119:9 Amp).

<u>Revelation, Meaning, Comments, Examples, Supporting Scriptures:</u>

Live a clean life by paying attention to what God says. Remain pure by behaving as God's Word prescribes. We are to guard our lives and rule our lives by obedience to the Word.

The Word DOES

Converts the Soul

"The law of the Lord is perfect, converting the soul: the testimony of the Lord is sure, making wise the simple" (Psalm 19:7 KJV).

Convicts of Sin

"And it came to pass, when the king had heard the words of the book of the law, that he rent his clothes. And the king commanded Hilkiah the priest, and Ahikam the son of Shaphan, and Achbor the son of Michaiah, and Shaphan the scribe, and Asahiah a servant of the king's, saying, Go ye inquire of the Lord for me, and for the people, and for all Judah, concerning the words of this book that is found: for great is the wrath of the Lord that is kindled against us, because our fathers have not hearkened unto the words of this book, to do according unto all that which is written concerning us" (2 Kings 22:11-13 KJV).

"Also in the third year of his reign he sent to his princes, even to Ben-hail, and to Obadiah, and to Zechariah, and to Nethaneel, and to Michaiah, to teach in the cities of Judah. And with them he sent Levites, even Shemaiah, and Nethaniah, and Zebadiah, and Asahel, and Shemiramoth, and Jehonathan, and Adonijah, and Tobijah, and Tob-adonijah, Levites; and with them Elishama and Jehoram, priests. And they taught in Judah, and had the book of the law of the Lord with them, and went about throughout all the cities of Judah, and taught the people. And the fear of the Lord fell upon all the kingdoms of the lands that were round about Judah, so that they made no war against Jehoshaphat" (2 Chronicles 17:7-10 KJV).

*"And when they brought out the money that was brought into the house of the Lord, Hilkiah the priest found a book of the law of the Lord given by Moses. And Hilkiah answered and said to Shaphan the scribe, I have found the book of the law in the house of the Lord. And Hilkiah delivered the book to Shaphan. And Shaphan carried the book to the king, and

The Word DOES

brought the king word back again, saying, All that was committed to thy servants, they do it. And they have gathered together the money that was found in the house of the Lord, and have delivered it into the hand of the overseers, and to the hand of the workmen. Then Shaphan the scribe told the king, saying, Hilkiah the priest hath given me a book. And Shaphan read it before the king. And it came to pass, when the king had heard the words of the law, that he rent his clothes. And the king commanded Hilkiah, and Ahikam the son of Shaphan, and Abdon the son of Micah, and Shaphan the scribe, and Asaiah a servant of the king's, saying, Go, enquire of the Lord for me, and for them that are left in Israel and in Judah, concerning the words of the book that is found: for great is the wrath of the Lord that is poured out upon us, because our fathers have not kept the word of the Lord, to do after all that is written in this book" (2 Chronicles 34:14-21 KJV).

<u>Revelation, Meaning, Comments, Examples, Supporting Scriptures</u>:

Read the entire chapter of 2 Chronicles 34 for King Josiah's response to the Law of the Lord.

Convinces

"Holding fast the faithful word as he hath been taught, that he may be able by sound doctrine both to exhort and to convince the gainsayers" (Titus 1:9 KJV).

Corrects

"All scripture is given by inspiration of God, and is profitable for doctrine, for reproof, for correction, for instruction in righteousness:" (2 Timothy 3:16 KJV).
   "...unto teaching, unto conviction, unto correction,..." (Rhm).
   "...for teaching the faith and correcting error, for resetting the direction of a man's life..." (Phi).
   "...for teaching, for refutation, for correction,..." (Mon).

The Word DOES

Defeats

"They defeated him by the blood of the Lamb and by the preaching of the Word;..." (Revelation 12:11 Nor).

Delights

"Your words are what sustained me; they are food to my hungry soul. They bring joy to my sorrowing heart and delight to me. How proud I am to bear Your name, O Lord" (Jeremiah 15:16 Tay).

Describes God

"Then said I, Lo, I come: in the volume of the book it is written of me," (Psalm 40:7 KJV).

Revelation, Meaning, Comments, Examples, Supporting Scriptures:

The Word describes God. It is His story. If you want to know God who is the Word, then read the book.

Detects

"...and detecting the inmost thoughts and purposes of the mind" (Hebrews 4:12 TCNT).

Educates in Righteousness

"Every holy Writing which comes from God is of profit for teaching, for training, for guiding, for education in righteousness" (2 Timothy 3:16 Bas).

Endures Forever

"The fear of the Lord is clean, enduring for ever:..." (Psalm 19:9 KJV).

The Word DOES

"The grass withereth, the flower fadeth: but the word of our God shall stand for ever" (Isaiah 40:8 KJV).

"But the word of the Lord endureth forever. And this is the word which by the gospel is preached unto you" (1 Peter 1:25 KJV).

Enlightens the Eyes and Mind

"The statutes of the Lord are right, rejoicing the heart: the commandment of the Lord is pure, enlightening the eyes" (Psalm 19:8 KJV).
    "...the Eternal's command is clear, a light to the mind" (Mof).
    "...The commandment of the Lord is intelligible, enlightening the mind" (Har).
    "...The commandment of the Lord shines clear and gives light to the eyes" (NEB).

Enlightens the Servant

"Also by them is Thy servant enlightened..." (Psalm 19:11 Sprl).

Exhorts, Encourages

"And after the reading of the law and the prophets the rulers of the synagogue sent unto them, saying, Ye men and brethren, if ye have any word of exhortation for the people, say on" (Acts 13:15 KJV).

"Holding fast the faithful word as he hath been taught, that he may be able by sound doctrine both to exhort and to convince the gainsayers" (Titus 1:9 KJV).
    "...able both to exhort in the healthful teaching..." (ABUV).
    "...able both to encourage with his healthful instruction..." (Rhm).
    "...competent to encourage others with wholesome teaching..." (Wms).

The Word DOES

"And I beseech you, brethren, suffer the word of exhortation: for I have written a letter unto you in few words" (Hebrews 13:22 KJV).

Revelation, Meaning, Comments, Examples, Supporting Scriptures:

In Hebrews 13:22, the word suffer, in other translations, means to bear, listen patiently, take kindly, and bear patiently.

Exposes

"...it exposes the very thoughts and motives of a man's heart" (Hebrews 4:12 Phi).

Forms

"By the word of the Lord were the heavens made; and all the host of them by the breath of his mouth" (Psalm 33:6 KJV).
    "At the bidding of the Lord the heavens were formed, and all their company at his decree" (Har).

Revelation, Meaning, Comments, Examples, Supporting Scriptures:

See Genesis 1, "In the beginning God..."

Framed the Worlds

"Through faith we understand that the worlds were framed by the word of God, so that things which are seen were not made of things which do appear" (Hebrews 11:3 KJV).
    "By faith we understand that the worlds [during the successive ages] were framed (fashioned, put in order, and equipped for their intended purpose) by the word of God, so that what we see was not made out of things which are visible" (Amp).
    "...that the ages have been framed by God's word,..." (ABUV).

The Word DOES

"...the ages to have been fitted together by declaration of God..." (Rhm).
"...that the worlds were prepared by the word of God..." (NASB).
"...that the world came into being by the command..." (Wey).
"...that the world was fashioned by the word..." (Mof).
"...that the worlds were put in order at God's command..." (Ber).
"...that the universe was created at the bidding of God..." (TCNT).
"...that the whole scheme of time and space was created..." (Phi).
"...created, beautifully coordinated, and now exist, at God's command..." (Wms).

<u>Revelation, Meaning, Comments, Examples, Supporting Scriptures</u>:

By faith (belief in the Word of God) I perceive and see that God is doing things we do not see. He is speaking words to change things and He is making something out of nothing, then we can see what He has made with our natural eye.

"...so that what is seen has not arisen out of things which appear" (Hebrews 11:3 ABUV).
    "...what we now see did not come from visible things" (Ber).
    "...what is seen does not owe its existence to that which is visible" (Wey).
    "...the world which we behold springs not from things that can be seen" (Con).
    "...To the end that not out of things appearing should that which is seen have come into existence" (Rhm).
    "...did not evolve out of existing matter" (Nor).
    "...and that they were made from nothing!" (Tay).

The Word DOES

Gives Guidance

"...for teaching, for refuting error, for giving guidance..." (2 Timothy 3:16 TCNT).

Gives Life

"...but it is on everything produced by command of the Lord that man lives" (Deuteronomy 8:3 AAT).
    "...but that man may live on anything that the Lord decrees" (Tor).

"...there is life for him in all the words which proceed from the mouth of God" (Matthew 4:4 Knox).

Gives Understanding

"I have more understanding than all my teachers: for thy testimonies are my meditation" (Psalm 119:99 KJV).

"I understand more than the ancients, because I keep thy precepts" (Psalm 119:100 KJV).

"Through thy precepts I get understanding: therefore I hate every false way" (Psalm 119:104 KJV).

"The entrance of thy words giveth light; it giveth understanding unto the simple" (Psalm 119:130 KJV).

"Let my cry come near before thee, O Lord: give me understanding according to thy word" (Psalm 119:169 KJV).

Gives Victory Over Satan

"Put on the whole armour of God, that ye may be able to stand against the wiles of the devil" (Ephesians 6:11 KJV).
    "You must wear all the weapons in God's armoury...the cunning of the devil" (Knox).

The Word DOES

"...and the sword of the Spirit, which is the word of God:" (Ephesians 6:17 KJV).
    "...and take the sword the Spirit wields..." (Wms).
    "...which is what God hath spoken:" (Rhm).
    "...which is the Message of God:" (TCNT).
    "...which is the voice of God:" (Gspd).

"Their victory was due to the Blood of the Lamb, and to the Message to which they bore their testimony..." (Revelation 12:11 TCNT).

<u>Revelation, Meaning, Comments, Examples, Supporting Scriptures</u>:

Jesus gained victory over Satan by speaking the Word:

"Then Jesus was led (guided) by the [Holy] Spirit into the wilderness (desert) to be tempted (tested and tried) by the devil. And He went without food for forty days and forty nights, and later He was hungry. And the tempter came and said to Him, If You are God's Son, command these stones to be made [loaves of] bread. But He replied, It has been written, Man shall not live and be upheld and sustained by bread alone, but by every word that comes forth from the mouth of God. Then the devil took Him into the holy city and placed Him on a turret (pinnacle, gable) of the temple sanctuary. And he said to Him, If You are the Son of God, throw Yourself down; for it is written, He will give His angels charge over you, and they will bear you up on their hands, lest you strike your foot against a stone. Jesus said to him, On the other hand, it is written also, You shall not tempt, test thoroughly, or try exceedingly the Lord your God. Again, the devil took Him up on a very high mountain and showed Him all the kingdoms of the world and the glory (the splendor, magnificence, preeminence, and excellence) of them. And he said to Him, These things, all taken together, I will give You, if You will prostrate Yourself before me and do homage and worship me. Then Jesus said to him, Be gone, Satan! For it has been written, You shall worship the Lord your God, and Him alone shall you serve" (Matthew 4:1-10 Amp).

The Word DOES

The Word of God is one of the weapons of the believer's armour. For a thorough understanding on the armour of God, read Ephesians 6:10-18.

Gives You an Inheritance

"And now, brethren, I commend you to God, and to the word of his grace, which is able to build you up, and to give you an inheritance among all them which are sanctified" (Acts 20:32 KJV).
  "...the inheritance..." (RSV).

Gives You Wisdom

"And that from a child thou hast known the holy scriptures, which are able to make thee wise unto salvation through faith which is in Christ Jesus" (2 Timothy 3:15 KJV).
  "...which can give you wisdom that leads to salvation..." (Wms).

Gives You Your Place

"...and to give you an inheritance..." (Acts 20:32 KJV).
  "...your place..." (TCNT).

Gives Your Proper Possession

"...and to give you an inheritance..." (Acts 20:32 KJV).
  "...your proper possession..." (Wms).

Gives Your Salvation

"...and to give you an inheritance..." (Acts 20:32 KJV).
  "...your salvation..." (Beck).

Good

"O thou that art named the house of Jacob, is the spirit of the Lord straitened? are these his doings? do not my words do good to him that walketh uprightly?" (Micah 2:7 KJV).

The Word DOES

"...Is the Lord short of patience, or are such his deeds? Do not my words promise good to him who walks upright?" (NAB).

"O house of Jacob, shall it be said, Is the Spirit of the Lord restricted, impatient, and shortened? Or are these [prophesied plagues] His doings? Do not My words do good to him who walks uprightly?" (Amp).

"Is that the right reply for you to make, O House of Jacob? Do you think the Spirit of the Lord likes to talk to you so roughly? No! His threats are for your good, to get you on the path again" (Tay).

Revelation, Meaning, Comments, Examples, Supporting Scriptures:

A loving Father disciplines those He loves with His Word (see Hebrews 12:6), for our good.

Guards

"When thou walkest, they shall guide thee; When thou liest down, they shall guard thee; When thou awakest, they shall talk with thee" (Proverbs 6:22 Sprl).

    "When thou walkest, take this along and let it be with thee: and when thou sleepest, let it guard thee; that when thou awakest, it may talk with thee" (Sept).

Guides

"When thou walkest, they shall guide thee; When thou liest down, they shall guard thee; When thou awakest, they shall talk with thee" (Proverbs 6:22 Sprl).

    "Wisdom, when you walk, will guide you, when you rest, she will take care of you, when you wake up, she will talk to you" (Mof).

    "When you go, they [the words of your parents' God] shall lead you; when you sleep, they shall keep you; and when you waken, they shall talk with you" (Amp).

The Word DOES

"Every holy Writing which comes from God is of profit for teaching, for training, for guiding, for education in righteousness" (2 Timothy 3:16 Bas).

Revelation, Meaning, Comments, Examples, Supporting Scriptures:

Proverbs refers to the Word as wisdom.

Heals

"He sent his word, and healed them, and delivered them from their destructions" (Psalm 107:20 KJV).
   "He sent out His word to heal them and to save their lives from the grave" (Ber).
   "He sent forth his word to heal them and to snatch them from destruction" (NAB).

Helps

"Let my soul live, and it shall praise thee; and let thy judgments help me" (Psalm 119:175 KJV).
   "…So shall thy regulations help me" (Rhm).
   "…long be your rulings my help!" (Jerus).

Imparts Saving Wisdom

"And that from a child thou hast known the holy scriptures, which are able to make thee wise unto salvation through faith which is in Christ Jesus" (2 Timothy 3:15 KJV).
   "…that can impart saving wisdom…" (Mof).

Instructs in Right Doing

"All scripture is given by inspiration of God, and is profitable for doctrine, for reproof, for correction, for instruction in righteousness:" (2 Timothy 3:16 KJV).
   "…and for instruction in right doing:" (Wey).

The Word DOES

Instructs in Righteousness

"All scripture is given by inspiration of God, and is profitable for doctrine, for reproof, for correction, for instruction in righteousness:" (2 Timothy 3:16 KJV).

Instructs You for Salvation

"And that from a child thou hast known the holy scriptures, which are able to make thee wise unto salvation through faith which is in Christ Jesus" (2 Timothy 3:15 KJV).
    "...to instruct you for salvation..." (RSV).

Judges

"He that rejecteth me, and receiveth not my words, hath one that judgeth him: the word that I have spoken, the same shall judge him in the last day" (John 12:48 KJV).
    "...The word that I spoke, that will judge him..." (ABUV).
    "...My spoken word, it shall sentence him..." (Ber).
    "...the word I spoke is what will judge him at the last day" (NASB).

"In the day when God shall judge the secrets of men by Jesus Christ according to my gospel" (Romans 2:16 KJV).

"For the word of God is living and active. Sharper than any double-edged sword, it penetrates even to dividing soul and spirit, joints and marrow; it judges the thoughts and attitudes of the heart" (Hebrews 4:12 NIV).
    "...and passing judgment on the thoughts and purposes..." (Wms).
    "...And able to judge the impulses and designs of the heart" (Rhm).
    "...and is skilled in judging the heart's ponderings and meditations" (Ber).

The Word DOES

Keeps from Paths of the Destroyer

"Concerning the works of men, by the word of thy lips I have kept me from the paths of the destroyer" (Psalm 17:4 KJV).

Revelation, Meaning, Comments, Examples, Supporting Scriptures:

"As for the doings of men, By the word of Thy lips I have shunned the paths of oppressors" (Psalm 17:4 DeW).
  "With regard to the works of men, by the word of thy lips I have avoided the ways of the violent" (RSV).
  "Through Your solemn decrees I have avoided lawless behavior" (Har).
  "according to the words of your lips I have kept the ways of the law" (NAB).

Keeps from Shame

"Then shall I not be ashamed, when I have respect unto all thy commandments" (Psalm 119:6 KJV).
  "Then shall I not be put to shame [by failing to inherit Your promises] when I have respect to all Your commandments" (Amp).
  "If I concentrate on your every commandment, I can never be put to shame" (Jerus).

Keeps Us

"When thou goest, it shall lead thee; when thou sleepest, it shall keep thee; and when thou awakest, it shall talk with thee" (Proverbs 6:22 KJV).
  "When you walk, let them follow you; let them be with you, keep them that they may keep you; and when you awake, meditate on them" (Lam).

The Word DOES

Keeps Watch on Us

"How shall a young man cleanse his way? By taking heed and keeping watch [on himself] according to Your word [conforming his life to it]" (Psalm 119:9 Amp).

"In thy going up and down, it leadeth thee, In thy lying down, it watcheth over thee, And thou hast awaked—it talketh with thee" (Proverbs 6:22 YLT).
> *"When you are walking about, it will lead you; when you are lying down, it will watch over you; and when you awake, it will speak to you"* (Ber).

Kills

"This is why I have cut them down by the prophets, and killed them by the words of my mouth..." (Hosea 6:5 Phi).

<u>Revelation, Meaning, Comments, Examples, Supporting Scriptures</u>:

Because the Word is a sword, it is a weapon that slays, kills and tears, among all the other things in this chapter. We must be skillful wielders of the sword to accomplish what God intends.

"And he had in his right hand seven stars: and out of his mouth went a sharp twoedged sword: and his countenance was as the sun shineth in his strength" (Revelation 1:16 KJV).

"Repent; or else I will come unto thee quickly, and will fight against them with the sword of my mouth" (Revelation 2:16 KJV).
> *"...and contend with such men with words that will cut like a sword"* (TCNT).

"And out of his mouth goeth a sharp sword, that with it he should smite the nations: and he shall rule them with a rod of iron: and he treadeth the winepress of the fierceness and wrath of Almighty God" (Revelation 19:15 KJV).

The Word <u>IS</u> The Word <u>DOES</u>

The Word DOES

Leads

"When thou goest, it shall lead thee; when thou sleepest, it shall keep thee; and when thou awakest, it shall talk with thee" (Proverbs 6:22 KJV).
> "In thy going up and down, it leadeth thee,..." (YLT).
> "When you are walking about, it will lead you;..." (Ber).

Leads to Obedience and Faith

"But now is made manifest, and by the scriptures of the prophets, according to the commandment of the everlasting God, made known to all nations for the obedience of faith:" (Romans 16:26 KJV).
> "...and at the command of the eternal God made known through the writings of the prophets to all the heathen to lead them to obedience and faith:" (Gspd).

Liberates

"And I will walk at liberty: for I seek thy precepts" (Psalm 119:45 KJV).
> "So, having sought your precepts, I shall walk in all freedom" (Jerus).

Makes

"By the word of the Lord were the heavens made; and all the host of them by the breath of his mouth" (Psalm 33:6 KJV).
> "By the word of Yahweh the heavens were made, their whole array by the breath of his mouth" (Jerus).

Makes Disciples of Christ

"Then said Jesus to those Jews which believed on him, If ye continue in my word, then are ye my disciples indeed;" (John 8:31 KJV).
> "...If ye abide in my word..." (ASV).
> "...If you live in My Word..." (Beck).
> "...If you are faithful to what I have said..." (Phi).

The Word DOES

"...As for you, if you hold fast to my teaching..." (Wey).
"...If you adhere to My teaching..." (Ber).
"...If you dwell within the revelation I have brought..." (NEB).

Revelation, Meaning, Comments, Examples, Supporting Scriptures:

We are tangible results of what the Word does when we believe.

Makes One Happy

"The statutes of the Lord are right, rejoicing the heart: the commandment of the Lord is pure, enlightening the eyes" (Psalm 19:8 KJV).
   "The teachings of the Lord are true, making one happy..." (Har).

Makes One Wise unto Salvation

"And that from a child thou hast known the holy scriptures, which are able to make thee wise unto salvation through faith which is in Christ Jesus" (2 Timothy 3:15 KJV).
   "...that can impart saving wisdom..." (Mof).
   "...and it is these that make you wise to accept God's salvation..." (Tay).

Makes Wise the Simple

"The law of the Lord is perfect, converting the soul: the testimony of the Lord is sure, making wise the simple" (Psalm 19:7 KJV).

Revelation, Meaning, Comments, Examples, Supporting Scriptures:

"...making wise the foolish" (Psalm 19:7 Sprl).
   "...making the ignorant wise" (Har).

The Word DOES

Makes You Strong

"And now, brethren, I commend you to God, and to the word of his grace, which is able to build you up, and to give you an inheritance among all them which are sanctified" (Acts 20:32 KJV).
  "…to make you strong…" (Bas).

Revelation, Meaning, Comments, Examples, Supporting Scriptures:

Jesus is the Word who accomplishes all the Word does.

Makes You Wise

"Therefore whosoever heareth these sayings of mine, and doeth them, I will liken him unto a wise man, which built his house upon a rock:" (Matthew 7:24 KJV).

"Let the word of Christ dwell in you richly in all wisdom; teaching and admonishing one another in psalms and hymns and spiritual songs, singing with grace in your hearts to the Lord" (Colossians 3:16 KJV).
  "Let Christ's teaching live in your hearts, making you rich in the true wisdom;…" (Phi).
  "Remember what Christ taught and let His words enrich your lives and make you wise;…" (Tay).

"And that from a child thou hast known the holy scriptures, which are able to make thee wise unto salvation through faith which is in Christ Jesus" (2 Timothy 3:15 KJV).
  "…and it is these that make you wise to accept God's salvation…" (Tay).

Never Fails

"…The Lord's instruction never fails,…" (Psalm 19:7 NEB).

The Word DOES

Nourishes

"If thou put the brethren in remembrance of these things, thou shalt be a good minister of Jesus Christ, nourished up in the words of faith and of good doctrine, whereunto thou hast attained" (1 Timothy 4:6 KJV).

"...Nourishing thyself with the words of the faith and of the noble teaching,..." (Rhm).

Overcomes

"And they overcame him by the blood of the Lamb, and by the word of their testimony; and they loved not their lives unto the death" (Revelation 12:11 KJV).

Penetrates

"...penetrating to the dividing line of the breath of life (soul) and [the immortal] spirit,..." (Hebrews 4:12 Amp).

"...it penetrates deeply, making a distinction between..." (Nor).

Perfects

"All scripture is given by inspiration of God, and is profitable for doctrine, for reproof, for correction, for instruction in righteousness: That the man of God may be perfect, thoroughly furnished unto all good works" (2 Timothy 3:16-17 KJV).

Pierces

"For the word of God is quick, and powerful, and sharper than any twoedged sword, piercing even to the dividing asunder of soul and spirit, and of the joints and marrow, and is a discerner of the thoughts and intents of the heart" (Hebrews 4:12 KJV).

"...It pierces even to the severance of soul from spirit,..." (Wey).

The Word DOES

<u>Revelation, Meaning, Comments, Examples, Supporting Scriptures</u>:

This is demonstrated in Acts 2:14-37.

"Now when they heard this, they were pierced to the heart, and said to Peter and the rest of the apostles, 'Brethren, what shall we do?'" (Acts 2:37 NASB).

Prevents Sin

"Thy word have I hid in mine heart, that I might not sin against thee" (Psalm 119:11 KJV).

"I have refrained my feet from every evil way, that I might keep thy word" (Psalm 119:101 KJV).

Produces Faith

"So then faith cometh by hearing, and hearing by the word of God" (Romans 10:17 KJV).
   "So faith comes from hearing what is told, and that hearing comes through the message about Christ" (Gspd).
   "We conclude that faith is awakened by the message…" (NEB).

Produces Hope

"For whatsoever things were written aforetime were written for our learning, that we through patience and comfort of the scriptures might have hope" (Romans 15:4 KJV).
   "…that by steadfast endurance, and by the counsel of the Scriptures, we may hold fast our hope" (Con).

Produces Power

"What we told you produced a powerful effect upon you, for the Holy Spirit gave you great and full assurance that what we said was true;…" (1 Thessalonians 1:5 Tay).

The Word DOES

Promotes Growth

"As newborn babes, desire the sincere milk of the word, that ye may grow thereby:" (1 Peter 2:2 KJV).

Promotes Spiritual Vigor

"The law of the Lord is perfect, converting the soul: the testimony of the Lord is sure, making wise the simple" (Psalm 19:7 KJV).
    "...promoting spiritual vigor;..." (Har).

Provides Doctrine

"All scripture is given by inspiration of God, and is profitable for doctrine, for reproof, for correction, for instruction in righteousness:" (2 Timothy 3:16 KJV).

Provides Moral Discipline

"All scripture is given by inspiration of God, and is profitable for doctrine, for reproof, for correction, for instruction in righteousness:" (2 Timothy 3:16 KJV).
    "...and for moral discipline:" (Mof).

Refreshes the Soul

"The law of the Lord is perfect, converting the soul: the testimony of the Lord is sure, making wise the simple" (Psalm 19:7 KJV).
    "...refreshing the soul..." (NAB).

Refutes

"Every Scripture is God-inspired and is helpful for teaching, for refuting error, for giving guidance,..." (2 Timothy 3:16 TCNT).

The Word DOES

Regenerates

"You have been regenerated (born again), not from a mortal origin (seed, sperm), but from one that is immortal by the ever living and lasting Word of God" (1 Peter 1:23 Amp).

Rejoices the Heart

"The statutes of the Lord are right, rejoicing the heart: the commandment of the Lord is pure, enlightening the eyes" (Psalm 19:8 KJV).

"Thy testimonies have I taken as an heritage for ever: for they are the rejoicing of my heart" (Psalm 119:111 KJV).
    "Thy testimonies have I claimed as mine heritage for ever; and why? they are the very joy of my heart" (PBV).

Renews Life

"The law of the Lord is perfect, converting the soul: the testimony of the Lord is sure, making wise the simple" (Psalm 19:7 KJV).
    "...renewing the life..." (AAT).

Reproves

"All scripture is given by inspiration of God, and is profitable for doctrine, for reproof, for correction, for instruction in righteousness:" (2 Timothy 3:16 KJV).

Resets the Direction of a Man's Life

"...for teaching the faith and correcting error, for resetting the direction of a man's life and training him in good living:" (2 Timothy 3:16 Phi).

The Word DOES

Restores the Soul

"The law of the Lord is perfect, converting the soul: the testimony of the Lord is sure, making wise the simple" (Psalm 19:7 KJV).
    "...restoring the soul..." (RV).

Revives Life

"The law of the Lord is perfect, converting the soul: the testimony of the Lord is sure, making wise the simple" (Psalm 19:7 KJV).
    "...reviving life..." (Mof).

"My spirit clings to the dust; Revive me according to thy word" (Psalm 119:25 AAT).
    "My soul is bowed to the dust: revive me, even as thou hast promised" (Mof).
    "I am completely discouraged—I lie in the dust. Revive me by your Word" (Tay).

"They give me strength in all my troubles: how they refresh and revive me!" (Psalm 119:50 Tay).

"I will never lay aside your laws, for you have used them to restore my joy and health" (Psalm 119:93 Tay).

Rules the Heart

"his steps never falter, because the law of God rules in his heart" (Psalm 37:31 Knox).

<u>Revelation, Meaning, Comments, Examples, Supporting Scriptures:</u>

The Word in the heart makes us want to do His Will.

"I delight to do thy will, O my God: yea, thy law is within my heart" (Psalm 40:8 KJV).

The Word DOES

Runs

"He sendeth forth his commandment upon earth: his word runneth very swiftly" (Psalm 147:15 KJV).

"See how he issues his command to the earth, how swift his word runs!..." (Psalm 147:18 Knox).

Sanctifies

"Sanctify them through thy truth: thy word is truth" (John 17:17 KJV).

"That he might sanctify and cleanse it with the washing of water by the word," (Ephesians 5:26 KJV).

Saves

"Wherefore lay apart all filthiness and superfluity of naughtiness, and receive with meekness the engrafted word, which is able to save your souls" (James 1:21 KJV).

Revelation, Meaning, Comments, Examples, Supporting Scriptures:

To be saved means to be born again in Jesus Christ.

"Being born again, not of corruptible seed, but of incorruptible, by the word of God, which liveth and abideth for ever" (1 Peter 1:23 KJV).

Scrutinizes

"For the Logos of God is a living thing, active and more cutting than any sword with double edge...scrutinizing the very thoughts and conceptions of the heart" (Hebrews 4:12 Mof).

The Word DOES

Shines Clear

"…The commandment of the Lord shines clear and gives light to the eyes" (Psalm 19:8 NEB).

Sifts

"…It sifts the purposes and thoughts of the heart" (Hebrews 4:12 NEB).

Slays

"O Ephraim, what shall I do unto thee? O Judah, what shall I do unto thee? for your goodness is as a morning cloud, and as the early dew it goeth away. Therefore have I hewed them by the prophets; I have slain them by the words of my mouth: and thy judgments are as the light that goeth forth" (Hosea 6:4-5 KJV).

"Therefore have I cut off the prophets, I have slain them by the words of my mouth…" (Lam).

<u>Revelation, Meaning, Comments, Examples, Supporting Scriptures</u>:

Because the Word is a Sword, it is a weapon that slays, kills and tears, among all the other things in this chapter. We must be skillful wielders of the Sword to accomplish what God intends.

Speaks to Us

"When you are walking about, it will lead you; when you are lying down, it will watch over you; and when you awake, it will speak to you" (Proverbs 6:22 Ber).

Sustains

*"Your words are what sustained me; they are food to my hungry soul. They bring joy to my sorrowing heart and delight

The Word DOES

to me. How proud I am to bear Your name, O Lord" (Jeremiah 15:16 Tay).

"But He replied, It has been written, Man shall not live and be upheld and sustained by bread alone, but by every word that comes forth from the mouth of God" (Matthew 4:4 Amp).

Takes Care of You

"Wisdom, when you walk, will guide you, when you rest, she will take care of you, when you wake up, she will talk to you" (Proverbs 6:22 Mof).

Talks with Us

"When thou goest, it shall lead thee; when thou sleepest, it shall keep thee; and when thou awakest, it shall talk with thee" (Proverbs 6:22 KJV).
 "...When thou awakest, they shall talk with thee" (Sprl).
 "...And thou hast awaked—it talketh with thee" (YLT).
 "...and when you awake, it will speak to you" (Ber).
 "...when thou awakest, it may talk with thee" (Sept).
 "...when you wake up, she will talk to you" (Mof).

Teaches

"Moreover, by them is thy servant taught;..." (Psalm 19:11 PBV).

"Let the word of Christ dwell in you richly in all wisdom; teaching and admonishing one another in psalms and hymns and spiritual songs, singing with grace in your hearts to the Lord" (Colossians 3:16 KJV).

"...for teaching, for reproof, for amendment,..." (2 Timothy 3:16 Mof).
 "...for teaching, for refutation, for correction,..." (Mon).
 "...for teaching, for refuting error, for giving guidance,..." (TCNT).
 "...for teaching, for training, for guiding,..." (Bas).

The Word DOES

Teaches the Faith

"...for teaching the faith and correcting error, for resetting the direction of a man's life and training him in good living:" (2 Timothy 3:16 Phi).

Tears

"O Ephraim, what shall I do unto thee? O Judah, what shall I do unto thee? for your goodness is as a morning cloud, and as the early dew it goeth away. Therefore have I hewed them by the prophets; I have slain them by the words of my mouth: and thy judgments are as the light that goeth forth" (Hosea 6:4-5 KJV).
   "...Therefore have I lashed you through the prophets and torn you to shreds with my words..." (NEB).

<u>Revelation, Meaning, Comments, Examples, Supporting Scriptures</u>:

Because the Word is a Sword, it is a weapon that slays, kills and tears, among all the other things in this chapter. We must be skillful wielders of the Sword to accomplish what God intends.

Testifies (Writes, Tells) of Jesus Christ

"And beginning at Moses and all the prophets, he expounded unto them in all the scriptures the things concerning himself" (Luke 24:27 KJV).

"Search the scriptures; for in them ye think ye have eternal life: and they are they which testify of me" (John 5:39 KJV).

"For he mightily convinced the Jews, and that publicly, shewing by the scriptures that Jesus was Christ" (Acts 18:28 KJV).
   "...proving by..." (TCNT).
   "...making clear from the holy Writings..." (Bas).
   "...quoting from the scriptures to prove..." (Phi).

The Word DOES

"...as he showed from the Bible..." (Beck).

"For I delivered unto you first of all that which I also received, how that Christ died for our sins according to the scriptures;" (1 Corinthians 15:3 KJV).

"...(the writing in the scroll of the book tells about Me)..." (Hebrews 10:7 Beck).
    "...just as the Scripture writes about me in the book..." (Wms).

Trains

"Every holy Writing which comes from God is of profit for teaching, for training, for guiding, for education in righteousness:" (2 Timothy 3:16 Bas).

Trains in Good Living

"All scripture is given by inspiration of God, and is profitable for doctrine, for reproof, for correction, for instruction in righteousness:" (2 Timothy 3:16 KJV).
    "...and training him in good living:" (Phi).

Trains in Uprightness

"All scripture is given by inspiration of God, and is profitable for doctrine, for reproof, for correction, for instruction in righteousness:" (2 Timothy 3:16 KJV).
    "...and in training in uprightness:" (Gspd).

Warns the Servant

"Moreover by them is thy servant warned: and in keeping of them there is great reward" (Psalm 19:11 KJV).

"...and were recorded for our benefit as a warning,..." (1 Corinthians 10:11 NEB).

The Word DOES

Watches Over You

"When you are walking about, it will lead you; when you are lying down, it will watch over you; and when you awake, it will speak to you" (Proverbs 6:22 Ber).

Works Effectively in Believers

"Let the word of Christ dwell in you richly in all wisdom; teaching and admonishing one another in psalms and hymns and spiritual songs, singing with grace in your hearts to the Lord" (Colossians 3:16 KJV).

"For this cause also thank we God without ceasing, because, when ye received the word of God which ye heard of us, ye received it not as the word of men, but as it is in truth, the word of God, which effectually worketh also in you that believe" (1 Thessalonians 2:13 KJV).

"...Which is also inwardly working itself in you who believe" (Rhm).

"...which has living power in you who have faith" (Bas).

"...[exercising its superhuman power in those who adhere to and trust in and rely on it]" (Amp).

"...which is even now doing its work within you who believe in Christ" (TCNT).

INDEX

Abiding	1
Accomplishes God's Will and Purpose	62
Adds Life, Prosperity, Peace	62
Admonishes	63
Advisor	1
Agreement	1
Answers Our Requests	63
Beautiful	1
Benefits	64
Blessing to Those Who Keep It	1
Blessing to Those Who Read and Hear It	2
Blessing to Those Who Seek Him with the Whole Heart	2
Blessing to Those Who Walk in It	3
Book of Prophecy	3
Book of the Law	3
Book of the Lord	3
Brings Joy	64
Broad	4
Builds Up Character	64
Builds You Up	64
Cause for Praise, Songs, Rejoicing	4
Causes One to Believe Jesus is the Christ, the Son of God	64
Causes One to Do No Iniquity and to Do No Unrighteousness	65
Cautions	65
Cleanses	65
Clear	5
Code	6
Comfort	6
Comforting	7
Comforts and Consoles	66
Commandment	7
Compact	7
Complete	7
Conforms Your Life	66
Consoling	8
Content of My Heart	8
Converts the Soul	67
Convicts of Sin	67

The Word IS The Word DOES

Convinces	68
Corrects	68
Counsellors	8
Course	8
Covenant	8
Defeats	69
Delight, Delights	9, 69
Deliverance	10
Describes God	69
Desired More than Gold	10
Detects	69
Discerner	11
Divine	11
Divinely-inspired	11
Educates in Righteousness	69
Effectual	11
Encourages	70
Endures Forever	69
Enduring	11
Energetic	12
Engrafted	12
Enlightens the Eyes and Mind	70
Enlightens the Servant	70
Ennobling	12
Established	12
Eternal (Forever)	12
Exalted	13
Examples	14
Exhorts	70
Exposes	71
Faithful	14
Favourable	15
Fire	15
Flawless	15
Flesh	15
Food (Bread, Milk, Nourishment)	16
Forms	71
Framed the Worlds	71
Fulfilled in Jesus Christ	16
Genuine	17
Gives Guidance	73
Gives Life	73

Gives Understanding	73
Gives Victory Over Satan	73
Gives You an Inheritance	75
Gives You Wisdom	75
Gives You Your Place	75
Gives Your Proper Possession	75
Gives Your Salvation	75
God (Logos, Divine, Christ)	17
God-breathed	18
God-inspired	18
God's Favor	19
God's Grace	19
God's Judgements	19
God's Law	19
God's Power	20
God's Testimonies	21
God's Way	22
Good	22, 75
Good News	22
Good Sense	23
Gospel	23
Gospel (The Good News)	23
Gracious	24
Great Reward	24
Guards	76
Guide, Guides	25, 76
Hammer	25
Healing	25
Heals	77
Health	25
Help, Helps	26, 77
Heritage	26
Holy	26
Hope	27
Human Being	27
Imparts Saving Wisdom	77
Instructions	28
Instructs in Right Doing	77
Instructs in Righteousness	78
Instructs You for Salvation	78
Intelligence	29
Intelligible	29

Joy	29
Judges	78
Just	30
Keener than the Sharpest Two-Edged Sword	30
Keeps from Paths of the Destroyer	79
Keeps from Shame	79
Keeps Us	79
Keeps Watch on Us	80
Kills	80
Kind	30
Knowledge	30
Lamp	30
Lasting	31
Law	31
Leads	81
Leads to Obedience and Faith	81
Liberates	81
Liberating	32
Life	32
Light	34
Living	35
Lovable	35
Magnified	35
Makes	81
Makes Disciples of Christ	81
Makes One Happy	82
Makes One Wise unto Salvation	82
Makes Wise the Simple	82
Makes You Strong	83
Makes You Wise	83
Meditation	36
Message of God	36
Message of God's Love	37
Message of Jesus Christ	37
Mystery	37
Name of Jesus	38
Near	38
Never Fails	83
Nourishes	84
Old	38
Operative	39
Orders of God's Lips	39

The Word IS The Word DOES

Overcomes	84
Path	39
Pattern for Living	8
Peace	40
Penetrates	84
Penetrating	40
Perfect, Perfects	40, 84
Pierces	84
Piercing	41
Pleasant	41
Pleasure	41
Powerful	41
Prevention from Sin	42
Prevents Sin	85
Produces Faith	85
Produces Hope	85
Produces Power	85
Profitable	42
Promotes Growth	86
Promotes Spiritual Vigor	86
Prophecy	43
Provides Doctrine	86
Provides Moral Discipline	86
Pure	44
Quick	45
Refreshes the Soul	86
Refutes	86
Regenerates	87
Rejoices the Heart	87
Reliable	45
Renews Life	87
Reproves	87
Resets the Direction of a Man's Life	87
Restores the Soul	88
Revelation of God's Grace	45
Reviver	46
Revives Life	88
Right	47
Righteous	47
Righteous Altogether	47
Rules the Heart	88
Runs	89

Sacred	48
Salvation	48
Sanctifies	89
Saves	89
Sayings of God's Mouth	49
Scroll	49
Scrutinizes	89
Seed	49
Settled in Heaven	50
Sharper than Any Two-Edged Sword	50
Shines Clear	90
Sifts	90
Sincere	50
Slays	90
Sound Doctrine	50
Speaks to Us	90
Spirit	51
Spiritual Law	51
Steadfast	51
Strength	51
Sure	51
Sustains	90
Sweet	52
Sweeter than Honey and the Honey Comb	53
Sword	53
Sword of the Spirit	53
Takes Care of You	91
Talks with Us	91
Teaches	91
Teaches the Faith	92
Teaching	53
Tears	92
Terms of Deliverance	54
Tested	54
Testifies (Writes, Tells) of Jesus Christ	92
Trains	93
Trains in Good Living	93
Trains in Uprightness	93
Tried	54
True	54
Trustworthy	56
Truth	54

The Word IS The Word DOES

Undefiled	57
Understanding	57
Upright	47, 57
Useful	58
Voice of God	58
Warns the Servant	93
Watches Over You	94
Way	8
What God Has Spoken	58
Wholesome	58
Wisdom	59
Witness Against You	59
Wonder	59
Wonderful	59
Wondrous	59
Word of Christ	60
Word of God	60
Word of the Lord	60
Works Effectively in Believers	94
Writing of God	61

www.ingramcontent.com/pod-product-compliance
Lightning Source LLC
Chambersburg PA
CBHW050319010526
44107CB00055B/2309